Scars of War

Marilyn Swinson

For all who served,
Love Marilyn Swinson

iUniverse, Inc.
Bloomington

Scars of War

iUniverse books may be ordered through booksellers or by contacting:

iUniverse
1663 Liberty Drive
Bloomington, IN 47403
www.iuniverse.com
1-800-Authors (1-800-288-4677)

ISBN: 978-1-4620-2871-9 (sc)
ISBN: 978-1-4620-2872-6 (hc)
ISBN: 978-1-4620-2873-3 (e)

Printed in the United States of America

iUniverse rev. date: 07/19/2011

For the brave men and women of
Combat Airmen/Joshua's Troops
and for all who bear
scars of war
in body, mind, or spirit

Contents

Foreword

The memory of my first meeting with Marilyn Swinson is still fresh in mind, and for good cause. She and her steady, Nick, visited me at home in the spring of 2009 for a radio interview. Guess what? Not more than a moment or two later, we were discussing veterans of World War II. People sometimes quietly say, as if their father might hear them, "We don't get Dad to say much about it." The inference, of course, is that those memories are still too shocking to recall. As often as not, that's not the reason. I stopped telling war episodes after a couple of tries in the forties. It was soon evident from the blank stares of my listeners that I wasn't getting through to them. Why? It's clear: words can't deliver the emotions along with the story. Frequently, it came across flat. The blank stare is a kind of body language. Even so, after another few moments with Marilyn and Nick, I decided to give it a try. They listened quietly.

As I droned on for three or four minutes, I looked straight into her eyes. Believe it or not the blank stare never appeared. Nope, when my short story ended, she calmly replied, "Thank you for sharing that experience with us." But something else was there. Somehow, across the airwaves, I got the message: she identified with my frustration at not being able to transmit the intensity of the moment. She knows how we think. I relaxed. Maybe that's the secret of her special bond with war veterans. In that respect, along with many others, Marilyn Swinson is the blue ribbon winner in the hearts of her veterans.

This exceptional individual, whom I have known for just a little over one year, honored me with an invitation to share in her new venture, with this introduction to yet another of her impressive literary creations. I accepted her gracious offer with pleasure at the opportunity to represent fellow veterans, honoring their much-loved friend and kind benefactress of both personal and public good will. The subject matter of this latest book is one with which her readers are familiar. It commemorates veterans of all our nation's wars. Their high-risk exposure contributes to our precious freedom by preserving a peace-loving civilization, hopefully for generations to follow. There's no guarantee. Former president Ronald Reagan thoughtfully reminded us, "The potential rejection of democratic freedom is no further away than the next generation." How can we show appreciation? Marilyn Swinson shows us how: with enthusiasm!

In any discussion about soldiers, we can't very well do justice to the subject without mentioning what they do. For brevity's sake, I will use the term "soldier" generically, to apply to members of all branches of military service, whether Coast Guard, Air Force, Marines, Navy, or Army personnel. Soldiers are trained to engage an enemy in war, in armed conflict, for the purpose of defending the national interests of their country, when so authorized by duly elected political authority.

From one foot-soldier's perspective, the following opinions are based on personal observations about war that, even when debatable, appear to be appropriate to the times. I think they will be familiar to you.

1. War is the political option of last resort in settling disputes between contending parties, when intense political negotiations fail to find terms of mutual agreement, by consultation, that can support continuing peaceful relations. Soldiers are employed to fight the wars that are "declared" by politicians. A soldier's destiny in battle depends, to some extent, on compatible perspectives between the two.

2. It's unlikely that a war has ever been declared without its dissenters. Because of them, World War II was an extremely close call. It's a fairly safe speculation to say that had Japan not been overly ambitious in its aggressor role, the isolationists

would have prevented US support of Europe, in which case democracy and freedom could by now be faint memories of a past civilization.

3. Now, in our time, a growing segment of the Western population, led by academia, mainline media, and some religious denominations, likes to believe that advanced, cultural knowledge and development qualifies dialectic negotiation as a replacement for armed conflict in the dominant, global, peacekeeping role. Their noble, well-meaning, wishful thinking is somewhat premature when taking into account the universal exploitation of language as the primary tool of deceptive strategies. The time for this thinking may come about, but in our time we might credit another ex-US president, George W. Bush, for his recent, cogent comment to the party: "It's best not to let expectations run too far ahead of reality."

4. A classic example occurred in World War II. It was a close call. On September 30, 1938, Britain's prime minister, Neville Chamberlain, returned home after negotiations with German chancellor Adolph Hitler, bringing "good" news to the British king's jubilant subjects as follows: "We, the German Fuhrer and Chancellor, and the British Prime Minister ... regard the [Munich] agreement signed last night ... as symbolic of the desire of our two peoples never to go to war with one another again. We are resolved that ... 'consultation' shall be the method adopted to deal with other questions that may concern our two countries" (quotesandsayings/nevillesp. htm).

What an ideal solution! Prime Minister Chamberlain's words are precisely those that almost everyone in the world yearns to hear, as the reality of human life. This was the moment to assure his place in history forever as the original peacemaker-by-persuasion. Now, war was subdued to the benefit of all humanity, and he the instigator of peace.

On September 1, 1939, almost one year later, Germany invaded Poland, with whom Britain shared a mutual defense treaty. The prime minister's message in part was this: "You can imagine what a bitter blow it is to *me* that all *my* long struggle to win peace has failed" (BBC: Special Report, emphasis added).

Allied soldiers carried the main brunt of Germany's extra year of production of Panzer tanks, the superior 88-millimeter artillery piece, aircraft, and highly trained combat troops in all branches. Note that at the time, Germany was already geared for industrial weapons production in full force. Britain had to start from near scratch, and almost a year later: a near fatal delay. Today, more than seventy years later, many of our incumbent congressional representatives seem not to have learned from previous, grievous errors of judgment. In evolutionary time, a balance of individual and social values for all humanity is our hope. Evolving humanitarian principles are not revealed to all civilizations simultaneously. Human nature's default priority under duress is set to preserve peace with physical response to aggression.

Marilyn, I'd like to close with a confession. After you and Nick departed, following our agreement about this introduction, I closed the door and stood stock-still staring at a blank wall, uttering aloud, "What have I done?" Then I retired to my spacious office in a daze and sat down. I recall that it crossed what was left of my mind that I had lost it. I was in way over my head. How could I, on such short acquaintance, do justice to introducing a multitalented model of the vaunted X gender to readers, many of whom have known her for thirty years or more?

Your book of verse, *Taking the Long Way Home*, was on my worktable. I picked it up, still in a daze, and started reading and couldn't stop until I finished the last page. Thoughts that revealed heartfelt convictions echoed through my mind:

Someday ... Christ will come to claim His own.
Then I shall look upon my Savior's face
—And know, at last, I have come home ...

On reading that, I knew at once that we would never again be strangers: home is where the heart is.

Captain Alexander Worth, USA, Retired
Darby's Rangers, First Battalion

Preface

When Pete Comer, commander of Combat Airmen/Joshua's Troops, asked if I would be interested in writing a book about members of his veterans' group, I first thought, *Whoa! I write poetry; this is something altogether different.* But I admit I was intrigued. After all, I had cut my teeth on all those heartrending movies of the forties and fifties that blatantly romanticize war. "Yes," I heard myself say, "I would love to."

That was almost four years ago. Since then, I have talked with more than forty veterans. I have listened to eyewitness accounts of the Bataan Death March; Pearl Harbor; the Normandy invasion; the flag going up on Iwo Jima; the frigid Korean front, including Heartbreak Ridge and Pork Chop Hill; booby-trapped rice paddies; and suicide bombers, among others.

One thing I have learned: war is not romantic. It is bleeding and dying and holding a lifeless comrade in your arms. It is watching young, healthy bodies blown asunder. It is storming a beach through a hail of bullets. It is fighter planes spiraling from the sky and Americans being taken captive. It is fatigue and fear and yearning for home and family.

The subjects of this book are not matinee idols; they are *real* men and women, mostly from small towns in North Carolina, who, when called upon, willed themselves to perform heroic deeds. Thus, they helped preserve freedom for us all—but at what cost to them?

I shall never forget the World War II veteran who agreed, albeit reluctantly, to sit for an interview. He made it through the background material without difficulty, but when he started to describe parachuting into battle, he broke down in sobs—not *tears* but *sobs*. After sixty-five years, the memories remained too painful to share.

Neither shall I forget the Korean War veteran who declined my invitation to have his story included in the book, but telephoned a month later to say he had thought about it and changed his mind; it was time to talk about what had happened.

Vietnam veterans, often victims of denigration by their own countrymen, are the most hesitant to speak out. One says simply, "That's between me and God." Then there is the heartwarming experience of an Operation Iraqi Freedom II battalion chaplain who fashioned a baptismal from camouflage and sandbags to baptize GIs who accepted Christ in the battle-ravaged Diyala Province northeast of Baghdad.

I consider it an honor to have been entrusted with committing these important accounts to print. I have made every attempt to faithfully report the information given me. My fear has been that I would not do justice to events of such personal and historical significance. I pray I have.

Acknowledgments

This book would not have been possible without the support and patience of my husband, Nick, who put up with my long hours and late nights glued to the computer. Also indispensable was the technical assistance I received from my son, Joe, as he talked me through innumerable glitches with the aforementioned computer and then drove four hours to help me transmit the completed manuscript to the publisher. Sons Mike and Tim, daughter-in-law Tam, and grandsons Brock (also a writer), Caleb, and Jonah graciously tolerated my single-minded devotion to the task, listened to drafts of stories, and provided encouragement.

Special acknowledgment is due Pete Comer for suggesting I write *Scars of War*, thereby initiating one of the greatest experiences of my lifetime. He has given freely of his time to arrange interviews with veterans and to provide pictures for the book, including the author's picture.

My eternal gratitude goes to Mollie Williams for the countless hours she spent editing copy and making suggestions on sections that needed to be rewritten for clarity.

Also, I am deeply indebted to Lisa Cantrell, Carla Harper, Dena Harris, and Mollie Williams, a close-knit group of accomplished writers and friends: their generosity of insight, experience, and expertise helped me to become a better writer and made this a better book.

Finally, I thank Pat Ransone for providing the picture of her father, Howard Gurley, which appears on the front cover of the book, and to *all* the wonderful men and women who shared their war stories with me. You are my heroes.

Introduction

Combat Airmen of World War II, later renamed Veterans of America, traces its roots to a conversation between Reidsville pharmacist Andy Gaster and his customer Hilton Monsees. As they admired Gaster's scale model of a B-24 bomber like the one Monsees had flown during World War II, they hit upon the idea of getting a group of fellow veterans together to share war stories. They enlisted the help of Phil Newman, pilot with the Fifteenth Air Force, retired.

The group held its first meeting on December 6, 1995, during which time they decided that one of their missions would be to go into public schools and talk about World War II. Although the group no longer exists, during their years of service, they spoke to an estimated thirty-eight thousand students and faculty. Furthermore, Ken Samuelson, a volunteer interviewer, audiotaped members' personal stories and placed them on permanent display in the North Carolina Department of Archives in Raleigh ("History of Veterans of America").

On March 3, 2006, at Ellisboro Baptist Church in Madison, Darrell Brumfield, Pansy Collins, Pete Comer, Jerome Joyce, Frank Lauten, Bob Porter, and Hassel Priddy met to form a Veterans Bible Club. They had a twofold purpose: first, to provide opportunities for veterans to engage in fellowship, and second, to go into schools and churches and teach Biblical and contemporary military history. Pete Comer was elected commander; Frank Lauten, vice commander; and Darrell Brumfield, chaplain.

With permission from founders of Combat Airmen of World War II, the new organization decided to incorporate that designation into the name of their group. But they wanted to attract veterans from *all* branches of service, not just Air Force, so Chaplain Brumfield suggested they add "Joshua's Troops" to their title, in honor of that great warrior of Scripture (Joshua 5:13–11:23). Thus, they became known as Combat Airmen/Joshua's Troops. A board of directors was elected, bylaws were adopted, and rules for teaching in schools were outlined.

Meetings are held on the second Thursday of each month at 8:30 a.m., at the Dan Valley Community Center in Mayodan. After fellowship and breakfast—catered by Pat Ransone—there are short business meetings followed by relevant guest speakers. To date, the group has shared information and war experiences with schools throughout Rockingham County and southern Virginia. They have made field trips to the Bedford Memorial and Tank Museum in Virginia. Jonathan Safrit, a student at Virginia Military Institute, placed a wreath at the Tomb of the Unknown Soldier in their honor.

Comer explains that three types of membership are recognized by the group: active members pay dues and are eligible to become officers, life members pay no dues but have the same privileges as active members, and honorary members pay no dues and do not vote. Spouses of members fall under the last category.

Current active membership is as follows:

D. Conrad Alberty
John Bigelow
Preston Bolick
Darrell Brumfield
Richard Bryant
Earl Cardwell
Hal Carter
Dick Cartwright
Robert "Bob" Comer
Henry "Pete" Comer
Paul Collins

Olga "Dusty" Lathrop
Frank Lauten
James "Big Jim" Louden
Roy Little
Orville Mabe
Richard Mack
Thomas McCollum
Chuck McGathy
Jack Neal
Dick Pennstrom
Bob Porter

Rush C. Collins
Kenneth Crowder
Ray Dawson
Clyde Easter Jr.
Bill Freeman
Fred Gann
Dan Green
Jake Hopper
Earnest Jones
Berlin Joyce
Rudolph Joyce
Jimmie Kallam
James A. King Jr.
William T. Knight

Hassel Priddy
William Rager
Pat Ransone
Leon Rumley
Jonathan Safrit
J. Shelton Scales
Fred Shelton
Cathy Smith
Boyd J. Steele
Russell Stewart
Nick Swinson
Robert W. Walker
Tom Williams

The following accounts are the result of
one-on-one interviews between author and
subjects. Exceptions are duly noted.

Unless otherwise specified, all cities and towns
referenced are located in North Carolina.

Damon Conrad Alberty

You had to build a shelf around yourself
where nothing could penetrate.

T he year was 1942. Japanese soldiers clearing out gun pits came upon seventeen-year-old Conrad Alberty—tattered, barefoot, sick, starving. They shoved a bayonet into the teenager's face and directed him to the main road, where a burgeoning assemblage of ragtag prisoners awaited. They were taken to Mariveles, on the southern tip of Bataan, and divided into columns of one hundred. Japanese Lieutenant General Masaharu Homma, charged with delivering the prisoners to Camp O'Donnell in the Philippine province of Pampanga, discovered that there were far more captives than he had anticipated, too many to transport by truck. The only way to get them to the camp was to make them walk the ninety miles. Thus began the infamous Bataan Death March—a forced transfer of seventy-five thousand fatigued, malnourished American and Filipino prisoners of war, the brutality of which resulted in the death of more than ten thousand men. The trek—estimated by Japanese high command to take only a couple of days—lasted ten instead.

Almost sixty years later, Alberty sits across the table from me in the kitchen of his Mayodan home. His posture is arrow-straight, his eyes focused and penetrating. His voice tolls clear and strong as he recites, matter-of-factly, accounts of unimaginable brutality perpetuated on one group of human beings by another.

Alberty grew up in nearby Greensboro, in the home of an older sister. He remembers passing happy summers camping and fishing on Buffalo Lake with friends. The sixteen-year-old had watched the buildup to war with interest and decided that he needed to enlist. He told an Army recruiter he was eighteen, and because proof of age was not required, he was accepted. After undergoing basic training at Fort Benning, Georgia, he requested duty in the South Pacific, thinking he would be safer there than in Germany. "A lie will get you nowhere," he cautions, "and you can see where this one got me."

Alberty, attached to the Fifty-Seventh Infantry Scouts, was sent to the Bataan Peninsula, part of the Central Luzon region of the Philippines. There he was caught up in the Battle of Bataan, one of the last stands of American and Filipino soldiers before Japanese forces overwhelmed them. General Douglas MacArthur's orders had been to "hold until reinforcements arrive." The Battling Bastards of Bataan fought valiantly for four months. They were running out of ammunition, medicine, clothing, shelter, and vehicles. Forced to eat dog meat, monkeys, lizards, iguanas, and cavalry horses to survive, the weakened men grew increasingly ill, many dying from malnutrition, beriberi, malaria, or yellow fever, as well as from enemy fire. Finally, on April 9, 1942, in desperation, Major General Edward King Jr., commanding general of Philippine-American forces on Bataan, surrendered his remaining troops to the Japanese Imperial Army. This was the largest military defeat in American and Filipino military history.

One of Alberty's most poignant memories of the ill-fated journey was of seeing his sergeant lose control and strike a Japanese officer. "He was wrestled to the side of the road, bent over, and decapitated right there." Beheadings, slit throats, and random shootings were the norm, as were bayonet stabbings, disembowelments, rifle-butt attacks, and denial of food and water to crazed men, forced to march hours in tropical heat. Prisoners existed on a handful of dry rice and a half-cup of water per day. "We were so thirsty," recalls my host, "that some drank from caribou wallows—puddles of water where caribou roll to drive away flies and mosquitoes." The contaminated water provoked epidemics of dysentery and other illnesses.

The trail became littered with dead bodies and ailing men begging not to be left behind. Alberty continues, "If one prisoner attempted to help another, both were beaten or killed. Convoys of Japanese trucks sometimes ran over marchers who fell, and Japanese soldiers in jeeps routinely struck stragglers in their backs and heads with bamboo poles as they drove past. If Japanese officers became displeased with their own men, they killed them also, adding to the carnage."

At night, exhausted hostages collapsed by the side of the road. "You might get an hour's sleep, and then it was up and go again. I don't ever remember sleeping," marvels Alberty, who at that point was down to eighty-seven pounds. "You could smell the camp about ten miles before you got there." The air reeked of dead bodies, urine, and stench from two maggot-riddled straddle trenches—the only toilet facilities available for thousands of men, most suffering from diarrhea.

Many men arrived at Camp O'Donnell so ill they never recovered. There was no medicine to treat the rampant malaria, and dysentery was practically universal. Prisoners who survived the Death March were promptly stripped of all belongings: blankets, writing materials, knives, surgical equipment, and cigarettes—leaving only canteens and mess kits. If Japanese items were found in the possession of a prisoner, that man was executed immediately, the belief being that those things had been stolen from the body of a Japanese soldier. Alberty recalls, "Heads of slain prisoners were mounted on bamboo poles and placed where work crews had to pass them going to and from their assigned jobs."

The captives were housed by groups of fifty in bamboo shacks with dirt floors. Each prisoner was part of a ten-man team; if one tried to escape, the other nine were also killed. They slept in cubbyholes directly on the bamboo, their heads on pillows stuffed with rice husks. Personal belongings, such as mess kits, were kept inside their pillows. Every hour, a Japanese soldier, armed with rifle, bayonet, and flashlight, came by to make sure all were present.

"Around eleven o'clock each morning, we were given our only meal of the day—a half-cup of rice and fish soup," explains the former POW, who learned to soak rusty nails in water and ingest the liquid to get needed iron into his system. Water was in short supply—one spigot for twenty-five thousand men. "We would have to stand in line hours to get a half-cup of water; my mouth was always parched."

From Camp O'Donnell, Alberty was sent to nearby Cabanatuan Prison Camp and assigned to burial detail. Estimating he buried over twenty-eight thousand bodies, he remembers thinking, "This can't be happening." But it was. The remains were stacked on top of each other in mass graves, a cross-shaped marker indicating the number of corpses in the grave—usually one hundred. There were no ceremonies, and names of the victims were not preserved. "People are still trying to find out what happened to their loved ones," he concedes. "We took their clothes off; they didn't need them anymore. Everything had to be steamed in barrels to kill lice and remove contagion from body ulcers and disease before it could be reused. We nailed shoe tops to two-by-fours to create workable footwear."

When not on burial detail, Alberty worked in a vegetable garden outside camp. He was also part of a two-man detail assigned to flatten a hill to allow for construction on an auxiliary airstrip for Nichols Field. The work was excruciating and the hours long. The men, lethargic and weary, went about their work in a daze. "You had to build a shelf around yourself where nothing could penetrate," says Alberty. He adds with conviction, "We knew someday we would be free; we just didn't know when. We knew that the nation we represented would someday be powerful enough to take the Philippines back."

Eventually, Alberty, along with six hundred other prisoners, was crammed into the hold of an old coal carrier bound for Japan. For twenty-eight days, he sat in a puddle of coal dust, unable to move about, inhaling the foul air—rife with human waste and random filth— and subsisting on minimal amounts of food and water.

He wound up in a prison camp 118 miles north of Hiroshima, where he was forced to unload war materials for the enemy. On August 7, 1945—one day after the first atomic bomb fell—the Japanese camp commander, who had been educated at the University of California, Los Angeles, ordered all prisoners to line up before him: "Yesterday, an American plane, a B-29, dropped a cheese-eye, buckle-shaped bomb, and a city disappeared," he barked. "I should kill everyone of you sons-of-bitches!"

No one knew what to expect, but by the next morning, the Japanese had vanished, the prisoners free to go and come as they chose. Some grabbed rifles and began shooting everything in sight. "I didn't do that," insists Alberty. "I had seen enough killing." Dutch troops liberated the emaciated men on September 4, 1945. Alberty had been a prisoner for three years and six months. "The atomic bomb saved us!" he declares emphatically. "Word had already gone out that if America invaded Japan from Okinawa, every prisoner of war would be executed. Graves were being dug out back."

The emancipated North Carolinian was in the hospital for six months for recuperation and treatment. After that, he was given the option of full retirement with pay or duty anywhere in the world. He chose Rome, Italy, where he served with the military police. He retired in 1953, after earning the following awards and decorations: Infantry Combat Badge, Presidential Citation with Two Oak Leaf Clusters, Philippine Citation with One Oak Leaf Cluster, Bronze Star Medal with Oak Leaf Cluster, Purple Heart Medal with Oak Leaf Cluster, Good Conduct Medal, American Defense with Foreign Service Clasp, Pacific Asiatic Medal with Two Battle Stars, Philippine Defense Medal with Two Battle Stars, Philippine Resistance Medal, Philippine Wounded Soldiers Medal, United Nations Medal, Occupation Medal–Japan, Occupation Medal–Italy, Victory Medal, Philippine Liberation Medal, and Prisoner of War Medal.

Alberty settled in Mayodan to be near his sister, who had relocated there. He married the former Ethel Mooney, now deceased. He has one daughter and two grandsons. For twenty years, he operated a storefront ministry sponsored by the Moravian Church. During his tenure, food, clothing, and medicine were supplied to more than ninety thousand disadvantaged individuals. He also served seventeen years on the town council. He is often called upon to share his story. "I do so with the hope that others, especially young people, will understand and appreciate the sacrifices that have been made to ensure their freedoms," he tells me.

Asked how his years in captivity have impacted his approach to life, he leans back in his chair, takes a long breath, and replies, "Well, I can sit down and drink a cup of hot coffee, and that is worth more than a million dollars to me."

Harvey Alexander

*I had to fight for an education, fight for a job, and
fight for the right to fight for my country.*

L ife was not always easy for Harvey Alexander, growing up poor
and black in the ubiquitous racial bigotry of 1920s America.
His father earned $700 a year in the Georgetown, Illinois, coal
mines—barely enough to provide his nine children with the necessities.
Little Harvey learned early on that realizing his considerable potential
was going to be an uphill battle. Born with an exceptional mind,
photographic memory, and ample portions of ambition and tenacity,
the precocious youth was not content to "stay in his place," or as one
white teacher put it, "make someone a nice houseboy."

Alexander, one of only three black students in his integrated
elementary school, enjoyed learning; he never missed class. One snowy
November day, the fifth-grader walked barefoot to school, not yet having
gotten his winter shoes; his father was working his way through the
family, purchasing one pair each payday. Since there was no lunchroom
in the schoolhouse, at noon Alexander walked home through six inches
of snow. When he walked *back* to school after lunch, his teachers and
principal were so impressed they rewarded him with a new pair of shoes
and socks.

Alexander recalls, "I know it looked pitiful to see this raggedy boy
walking barefoot in the snow. But I want everybody to know that my feet
were not cold, and I did not suffer in the least. My feet had become so
acclimated to the cold by going all summer and into the winter without

shoes that it did not affect me one bit. But of course," he adds, "I was glad to get the shoes."

Other incidents *did* affect Alexander, however; he remembers being very hurt. Having always led the class academically, no one was surprised when he became valedictorian. But the honor, along with the thousand-dollar scholarship to Illinois College, was taken away from him and given to the next in line, a white girl. Alexander was demoted to salutatorian. Not only that, but when he was inducted into the National Honor Society and presented the Bausch and Lomb award for achieving the highest average in three years of science, it was in a private ceremony in the principal's office. Thirty white students received their awards the next week in a school-wide assembly, surrounded by parents, siblings, aunts, uncles, and grandparents. No mention was made of Alexander's achievements.

Alexander always told his parents, "I'm going to college."

"Okay," they would respond, thinking he would eventually realize the futility of his dream. But when their child's senior year rolled around, and he again said he was going to college, they asked, "Son, *how* are you going to college?"

Alexander had a plan: he went to work for the National Youth Administration (NYA), earning a quarter an hour. Meanwhile, he applied for a scholarship to Fisk University. They responded that they did not have a program for "working" students and referred him to Tuskegee Institute. But Alexander persisted, and with referrals from two former graduates, he obtained a freshman scholarship.

The eighteen-year-old set out for Nashville, Tennessee, clutching a one-way ticket purchased by his father, sixty-four dollars earned while working with the NYA, and a seventeen-dollar suit given to him for graduation. During breaks from class, he washed walls for money, and in the summer, he traveled to Detroit to work as fry cook on the SS *Buffalo*—a luxury ship sailing between Detroit and Buffalo. The brightest spot of his time at Fisk was when he met his future wife, Esther Beatty.

Following his sophomore year, Alexander decided to transfer to the University of Illinois School of Commerce, which offered advanced accounting and business courses. "The dean called me to his office so he could tell me in person that he was proud of being able to place all his graduates; he could never place me, and I would be wasting my time and his if I enrolled. He advised me to pursue a degree in agriculture. I told him that I was more familiar with discrimination in the state of Illinois than he was because I had lived it. I said there would be a time when these jobs would be available to Negroes, and if I didn't get the training now, I would not be ready when that time came." Alexander prevailed, becoming the first black student in the School of Commerce, but that was not his last encounter with discrimination.

On the first day of Cost Accounting, the professor paused after calling his name, looked at him, and proclaimed, "*Some* people need to understand that not everyone can be a cost accountant; someone has to sweep the factory floor."

In Business Letter Writing, his papers were returned marked "F" or "D," although no mistakes were highlighted. When the puzzled student asked what was wrong with his work, he was told, "It's too good; it can't be yours. You must have copied it."

"Give me an assignment," offered Alexander. "I will do it right here in front of you."

"No!" returned the professor. "And I can tell you right now that you are not going to pass this course." The dean of students arranged for Alexander to transfer to another class.

In Industrial Management, the instructor boasted that he was "free, white, and twenty-one, unlike *someone else* in the room." And in yet another class, the undergraduate was not permitted to ask or answer questions, nor could he speak with the teacher in his office. The next year, tired of denigration, the disillusioned but resolute young man transferred to the University of Michigan.

Seventeen days after beginning his studies at U of M, Alexander received his draft notice, ordering him to appear September 26, 1942—

ten days later. He hurried to Detroit to apply for pilot training. Upon acing the written and physical tests, he was held in Michigan to await transfer to the Air Corps. When orders had not arrived after thirty days, he was carried by troop train to Camp Atterbury, Indiana, where he was attached to the 92nd Buffalo Division, 369th Infantry Regiment, the same one his father had served with during World War I.

Because of his three years of college, Alexander was made acting sergeant, in charge of the machine gun section. He had a good rapport with his men, who looked up to him and worked hard to meet his standards. As a result, the machine gun section was the only unit on base to pass the core area test. "I was so wrapped up in what I was doing, and enjoying it so much, I forgot I had applied for pilot training," he admits. When his master sergeant found him in the field to tell him his orders had come through, Alexander had to stop and think about what he meant.

Alexander traveled to Keesler Field in Biloxi, Mississippi, for his second round of basic training. Having already served as a noncommissioned officer at Camp Atterbury, he was quickly placed in charge of recruit instruction. "I was gung-ho Army by this time," he says, "and infantry training is more strenuous than Air Corps. For a while I was the most hated man in camp because I insisted on doing things the Army way, but after the men got into shape, they came to appreciate me—*I think*."

At last, Alexander arrived at Tuskegee Air Field, the only training site for black military pilots. Once there, he was named senior cadet, a position he held until obliged to undergo minor surgery. During his two-week convalescence, he returned to Illinois and persuaded Esther to marry him. They wed in Cairo, Illinois, on December 19, 1943. The bridegroom received his wings and was promoted to second lieutenant on April 15, 1944. Having chosen to fly twin-engine, in hopes that would improve his chances of becoming a commercial pilot after the war, he was sent to Mather Field, Sacramento, California, to train on the B-25. Sadly, *no* Tuskegee Airman would ever be hired by a commercial airline. More disappointing at the time, however, was that no general in the US Army wanted black pilots. "We were considered mentally and physically unfit for flying," recalls Alexander.

Shunned, the Tuskegee Airman just kept flying, eventually logging 964 hours of flight time. In comparison, white pilots flew combat after accruing 20 to 35 hours. According to Alexander, "When black pilots were finally allowed to fly escort for fighter planes, due to the intervention of Eleanor Roosevelt, white cover pilots were losing thirty-five to sixty-five of every hundred planes they escorted. Tuskegee Airmen didn't lose a single plane in more than two-hundred missions." Alexander regrets that he never saw action; black pilots of twin-engine planes were never deployed.

Alexander loved to fly; at twelve thousand feet, he found freedom: "Those twin seventeen-hundred-horsepower engines churning on each side of the cockpit imparted their power into my very being. As I flew the skies over the United States," he exclaims, "I felt a sense of empowerment that was not present on the ground. There, I was in control and not subject to society's imposed restrictions of segregation and humiliation."

Esther lived and worked in Cairo, so when Alexander completed active duty, he reluctantly returned to the University of Illinois School of Commerce to be near her while completing his business degree. Unfortunately, the dean's earlier prediction came true; of the thousand-plus students graduating in 1947, he was the only one who had not been matched with a job. Nevertheless, he went on to enjoy a distinguished and rewarding career: he taught accounting at Southern University in Baton Rouge, Louisiana, and North Carolina Agricultural and Technical (A&T) University in Greensboro. He was business manager at Shaw University in Raleigh and at North Carolina A&T before accepting a position as vice president of business and finance at Johnson C. Smith University in Charlotte.

Once in Charlotte, he learned that the institution was in financial chaos. He cut five hundred unfunded scholarships and secured a two-million-dollar loan to keep the doors open. When he left, the school enjoyed a $750,000 surplus.

Alexander also served as vice president for business and finance at Pratt Institute in Brooklyn, New York, and at Tennessee State University in Nashville, Tennessee. Finally, he became owner and operator of Alexander Vending Enterprises in Nashville.

Fast forward to 2007: Alexander was presented the University of Illinois' highest award, the Presidential Medallion. There, before thousands of attendees, he was given a public apology for the way he had been treated as a student and recognized as the first black to enter and graduate their School of Commerce. The same year, he and more than three hundred Tuskegee Airmen were awarded Congressional Medals of Honor. This followed on the heels of his having been given an Honorary Doctorate of Public Service from Tuskegee University (2006).

The Alexanders have two daughters, Robin and Karen, and are proud great-grandparents. They live in Greensboro, in a beautiful home built by his own hands. "It's been a long and fulfilling life," he assures me. "I believe we helped pave the way for others."

Alexander's war memorabilia are displayed at the International Civil Rights Center and Museum at 134 South Elm Street, Greensboro.

John Bigelow

*That was my first kill; I was never so sick in my life as
the day I killed that boy. I'm sure the sharks got him.*

It was 1945, and seventeen-year-old John Bigelow, who lived next
door to the naval base in Jacksonville, Florida, was chomping at
the bit to get into the service. He didn't really care which branch;
he just wanted to fight the Japanese. Finally, he convinced his father
to sign for him to join the Navy. He survived basic training and was
enrolled in aircraft mechanic school.

In time, Bigelow was assigned to the Navy Hunter-Killer Squadron.
Their mission was to fly north from Jacksonville for about four hours and
return to base, all the while searching for German underwater submarines.
When they spotted one, they were to entice it to the surface, get the crew
on deck, and call in warships to make the capture. Once, they found a
hostile submarine on the North Carolina–South Carolina border in the
vicinity of Myrtle Beach. The vessel came to the surface as ordered; the
crew came up on deck. Bigelow and his comrades—in their twin-engine
seaplane—circled the enemy craft continuously in a counterclockwise
direction in order to keep their prey under surveillance. Suddenly, one
of the Germans grabbed a machine gun and turned toward his captors.
Bigelow, as portside gunner, was ordered to "splash" the young sailor.
"That was my first kill," he says. "I was never so sick in my life as the day
I killed that boy. I'm sure the sharks got him."

After World War II, Bigelow left the Navy, becoming part of what
he calls the "52-20 club." For fifty-two weeks, he was entitled to receive

twenty dollars a week to tide him over while he searched for work. He did try—unsuccessfully—to find a job. After a while, he decided that the best thing he could do was reenlist in the military. Accordingly, he went to the Navy recruiter and announced, "I'm all yours; you can have me."

To this the recruiter replied, "I don't want you. I have a waiting list."

"But I have to have a job," argued Bigelow.

"Well, the guys down the hall need one more man ready to leave in the morning," offered the recruiter. "Do you want the job?"

He did. But he soon found that "the man down the hall" was a *Marine* recruiter. Early the next morning, Bigelow left Jacksonville on a train bound for Yamassee, South Carolina. He says what he encountered there was "one tiny train depot, a Marine Corps bus, and one *bad* Marine."

The Marine kept yelling, "Get off that train! Move! Move! Move!"

"What's your hurry?" queried Bigelow.

"At that point," he admits, "I was introduced to the wooden platform. I didn't give him any more trouble. From then on, I did exactly what I was told. I was taken to Parris Island, where I spent ninety days in 'recruit training hell.' I was informed that there were only three ways off the island: suicide; through the quicksand, sharks, and alligators; or past the man at the gate with a forty-five on his side. I decided to tough it out."

After a short stay in Camp Lejeune, where he was trained as truck driver and mechanic, Bigelow was stationed at Norfolk, Virginia. His job was to chauffeur officers to and from various appointments—that is, until the North Koreans crossed the line into South Korea. Two days later, he found himself on a train bound for Camp Pendleton, California. From there, he sailed across the Pacific Ocean to Okinawa, where he became part of the Inspector General's team. He describes his assignment as "lying in mud under trucks in Korea, trying to make repairs while bullets bounced around my head" and "flying back and forth to Okinawa to obtain needed parts."

In December 1950, upon returning to Korea after a routine trip to Okinawa, Bigelow was told that he would not be going back to Okinawa;

his gear would be shipped to Korea, where it would catch up with him. "It never did," he recalls. "I was issued a vehicle, rations, ammunition, and a compass, then sent north to help liberate the Frozen Chosin, a division of Marines pinned down by two divisions of the Chinese Army." After the People's Republic of China entered the conflict, their troops swept across the Yalu River to encircle United Nations troops fighting in the northeastern part of North Korea at the Chosin Reservoir. Bigelow was part of an effort to get vehicles up there and bring out as many of the sick and wounded and as much equipment as possible.

Three-star general Oliver P. Smith commanded the trapped Marines. He was nicknamed Hollering Man Smith "because he was always mad and always hollering," explains Bigelow. "He refused to leave the Reservoir unless he could take all of his men and equipment with him. We were forced to use tanks, hoods of trucks—any space we could find that would hold men or gear—as we facilitated the breakout. At night, the temperature dipped to sixty-five degrees below zero; vehicles slid on ice and turned over into ravines. Many died as we made our way south to Inchon."

Asked if the Marines were retreating, General Smith stormed, "Retreat hell! We're not retreating; we're just attacking in a different direction." When they came within a half-mile of their destination, the general had his men "fall in," and they marched in singing the Marine Corps Hymn. Bigelow remembers being impressed by this display of courage.

He left Korea fourteen months later and made his way back to Norfolk, where a wonderful surprise awaited him. He shares, "I met the one person who means the most to me, the one person for whom I served in the military so long, trying to support and protect—my wife of fifty-eight years, Betty Jane Lowe Bigelow. She was in Norfolk caring for her niece's children, babysitting during the day and working at a soda fountain at night. I found her behind the counter, and thirty days later, we were married." The couple remained in Norfolk for about five years. During that time, Bigelow was sometimes away on short deployments, one of which was to Puerto Rico.

In 1957, Bigelow was again ordered to Okinawa, this time for fourteen months. He was attached to the Third Marine Division. From there he traveled to Luzon, in the Philippines, to participate in maneuvers. When those were completed, he was helping load the ship for the return trip when he noticed the moon on the side of the ship where he was standing. He went below for about an hour, and when he came back up, the moon was on the opposite side. He said to himself, "That doesn't happen too often; something is going on." He asked a Navy chief, "Why have we turned around and headed south again?"

"We're not going south," he snapped. "You're imagining things. Go down below."

An hour later, Bigelow learned that Indonesia was having a "little brush fire," and they were being sent there (south) to calm things down. "So," he reflects, "that was another combat action during which I was fortunate enough to be in the wrong place at the wrong time, or perhaps the right place at the right time."

Bigelow left Okinawa in 1960 and spent time patrolling the Mediterranean Sea. He explains that "after World War II, all Allied forces were supposed to take turns guarding the Mediterranean, but to date, only the United States has done so." The Sixth Naval Fleet is stationed there permanently, members serving six- to nine-month tours of duty.

He was eventually transferred to Camp Lejeune, where he was attached to motor transport school, with orders to teach basic electricity, magnetism, engine overhaul, and rebuilding. He did this for three years, eight hours a day.

He remembers a Marine captain interrupting one of his lectures, asking him to yield the podium. He stepped aside. The captain appeared shaken. "I hate to inform you," he began solemnly, "that our Commander-in-Chief has been killed in Dallas, Texas." He spoke, of course, of President John F. Kennedy's assassination. Bigelow recalls experiencing a great sense of personal loss.

Next, he was sent to Iwakuni, Japan, where he boarded an LST and proceeded to Chu Lai, Vietnam, to assist in building an airfield to be used for takeoffs and landings by American pilots battling the Vietcong. The major also served in Da Nang and along the Ho Chi Min Trail—a network of roads that ran from North Vietnam to South Vietnam through the neighboring countries of Laos and Cambodia.

In 1965, Bigelow was ordered to Greensboro to work with a reserve organization. For the next three years, he was responsible for notifying families in the surrounding area when their loved ones were killed, wounded, or missing in action. He also performed funerals and on occasion picked up individuals who were AWOL. These he carried to the Guilford County jail to be held until someone from Camp Lejeune came to pick them up.

Then in 1968, Bigelow was to be reassigned to Da Nang. He requested retirement instead. He reasons, "After twenty-two years, I just felt that my luck had run out. I would not make it home again." Although it was the time of the Chinese New Year, and a big push was expected in Vietnam, the military granted his request. He remained in Greensboro, working with Burlington Industries and Black Cadillac-Oldsmobile. He and Betty Jane make their home in Stoneville. They have two sons—Michael David and John James—and three grandchildren.

In 2002, Bigelow was diagnosed with lung cancer and consequently lost a lung. He acknowledges, "After that, I knew that I had to go to work for someone other than the Marine Corps or myself. I knew there had to be something else I could do with one lung, diabetes, and Agent Orange." His search led him to join Gideons International. For the past six years, he has been an active member of the Madison-Mayodan Camp, where he serves as treasurer.

Preston Bolick

[T]o the amusement of all present, a ship's
officer received 'the boot' from a swabby.

The war had ended months earlier, so why were Preston Bolick of Stoneville and three of his companions staring down the barrel of a rifle, struggling to explain to non-English-speaking soldiers what they were doing in a Chinese army camp—carrying shotguns?

Bolick had joined the Navy in April 1946. He took his basic training in San Diego, California, and from there went to Treasure Island, San Francisco, for shipment overseas. The seaman first class was assigned to the destroyer *Fred T. Berry*. After a stop in Hawaii, he sailed for Iwo Jima and later Okinawa; the crew did not go ashore at either location, but merely sailed around each. They did go ashore in Yokosuka, Japan—a bombed-out naval yard. Bolick was fascinated by the underground railroads located inside tunnels dug by the Japanese in their long preparation for war. Within these man-made conduits, Japanese craftsmen had equipped and repaired seagoing vessels. Bolick and his companions passed through the mountain into town, where the only building left standing after bombing had been turned into a USO club.

The *Fred T. Berry*'s next stop was Tsing Tao, China, headquarters for the Seventh Fleet. When in port, the sailors often went into Tsing Tao for liberty. "Where we were," remembers Bolick, "there was a great big bay, and beyond that bay, we could still see fighting and flashing, because as soon as the Japanese left, the Communists and the Nationalists resumed their fight." Certain areas were therefore restricted.

It was in Tsing Tao that Bolick met Tsui Chi Hsii, a small Chinese boy better known as Charlie Two Shoes, a nickname given him by the Marines of Love Company when they adopted him in 1945. "We performed target practice at the firing range, a huge mound of dirt rising several feet in the air," he explains. "The Chinese, being curious, came out to lie near the target area and watch the action, thus exposing themselves to possible danger. We tried a number of ways to persuade them to leave, but they would not. Finally, out of desperation, we asked Charlie to speak to them in Chinese and convince them to stay away for their own safety."

While still in Tsing Tao, Bolick and three friends decided to go hunting. They were instructed to give anything they caught to the Chinese and to be back on ship before dark. They tramped through the hills for a while without finding game. As they ventured deeper into the woods, shooting randomly at inanimate objects, they realized they were lost, and darkness was overtaking them. They crossed a deep ravine and climbed up the other side. Suddenly, they heard a voice. Looking up, they saw a Chinese soldier with a rifle pointed toward them, motioning them away. They turned back, retraced their steps, and came out the opposite side of the ravine. A short distance ahead, they encountered a barbed wire fence. Not knowing what to do next, they crawled through the barrier, inadvertently situating themselves *inside* a Chinese army camp.

The sailors saw another Chinese soldier walking guard and decided to approach him. As they did so, the startled soldier whirled around, bringing his rifle within inches of Bolick's face. The guard cried out for help: lights popped on in the barracks, and Chinese rolled out en masse, surrounding the helpless Americans. They marched their captives to the main gate, where they turned them over to an officer who spoke English.

"What in the world are you doing in this camp?" he demanded. After the sailors explained their plight, the officer assured them, "You're lucky you didn't get shot. If it had been *you* who found *us* in your camp, you would have shot first and asked questions later." The officer pointed to distant, barely perceptible lights. "*That* is the Gulf," he scolded. "That is where your ship is."

The admonished hunters set out again on foot in the freezing temperature. En route, they came across Dave's Bar and Grill, run by a Russian. As they entered the door, one of the sailors foolishly joked, "This is a stickup." After a tense, decidedly awkward pause, they were invited inside, where a pot-bellied stove provided welcome warmth.

The accommodating Russian invited his dancing girls to "sit on these boys' laps and help warm them up." Eventually, the men left the comfort of the bar and slogged their way back to the ship, where they were given a proper tongue-lashing and restricted to the ship for an extended period of time.

"I did one thing that not many enlisted men ever get to do," boasts Bolick. "I kicked an officer, the ship's doctor, in the seat of the pants and got away with it." When I ask for details, he relates the following story: "The doctor requested his mail. I told him that the mail carrier had not returned, but teased that no one would be writing him anyway. He bet me they would. Having no money, I wagered a kick in the seat of the pants that no mail would be forthcoming. He agreed, but assured me that he would not operate on me to get his foot out when I lost. Actually, I knew what he had forgotten; this was Sunday, so no mail would be delivered. Consequently, to the amusement of all present, a ship's officer received *the boot* from a swabby."

Bolick next sailed to Shanghai and then to Amoi, where his was the first American ship to dock after the war ended. He went ashore in Hong Kong—a British Crown colony at that time. There, British sailors mingled with their American counterparts. One observed, "You American sailors have it made. Even on a tugboat, you have a washing machine. When we wash clothes, we have to give it *the elbow*. And you have bunks. We swing a hammock wherever we can find room."

After a short stay in Guam for repair, the ship sailed for Pearl Harbor. On the way, Bolick decided to climb his gun mount, nestle in the bloomers, and take a short snooze. He awakened to the sound of crew members shouting out his name. "They were just before reporting me overboard," he says, laughing. "I paid for that nap with a severe dressing down."

The ship went into dry dock in Bremerton, Washington, for about thirty days to undergo scraping and repainting. Afterward, they returned to San Diego, where they learned that the *Fred T. Berry* would make another voyage to China. Bolick did not have enough time left in his hitch to accompany them without reenlisting, which he refused to do. He was therefore assigned to another destroyer, the USS *Wiltsie*. "The ship was in dire need of attention," he points out. "My first order of business was to remove the rust and get the forty-millimeter quads in working order."

After completing his term in the Navy, Bolick returned to Rockingham County. Eighteen months later, he married Gaynell Clark. The couple has three children: Donna Lynn, Curtis, and Mark. Bolick worked for ten years for Baxter-Kelly, a furniture manufacturer, before becoming a Rockingham County deputy sheriff, a position he held for twenty-six years. He and Gaynell, now retired, live in Stoneville, surrounded by children and grandchildren.

Darrell Brumfield

Sometimes we were hit by roadside bombs. At other times, after being hit by a bomb, we were ambushed and forced into a firefight.

C aptain Darrell Brumfield sits behind his orderly desk in front of a wall-sized bookcase laden with variously shaped books—primarily on theology. As he shares an abbreviated biography of his event-filled life, I am struck with his youthful appearance and confess that I supposed him to be much younger. He flashes a boyish smile and informs me that he "graduated seminary at Liberty University, Lynchburg, Virginia, in 1981." While there, he met Donna, his wife and mother of his two adult children, Daniel and Laura Beth.

Brumfield, who grew up in Reidsville, spent a decade as pastor of LaSalle Baptist Church in Niagara Falls, New York. He has been at his current location, Ellisboro Baptist Church in Madison, for the past seventeen years. While pastoring in New York, his church hosted a conference attended by a chaplain representative who spoke passionately of a shortage of military chaplains. The chaplain later contacted Brumfield and asked if he would consider serving. Consequently, Brumfield was commissioned after undergoing a year of background checks. "I served with the Army National Guard Infantry Brigade out of Buffalo, New York, until I came to North Carolina, where I became attached to the Thirtieth Infantry Brigade. I was activated in September of 2003 and joined the First Infantry Division in Iraq in 2004."

When the pastor/chaplain offered to resign his pastorate, church members asked him to remain in that position, but to engage an interim pastor. Dan Jones, a retired minister from Reidsville, was hired and stayed with them the sixteen months Brumfield was away. Donna and the children remained at Ellisboro. She distributed a prayer card, picturing Brumfield in his uniform, throughout the community. The family received overwhelming support and encouragement.

Brumfield was part of Operation Iraqi Freedom II (OIF2). His division served in the Diyala Province northeast of Baghdad. They were responsible for security from Tikrit to the Iranian border. Particular hotspots were Baqubah and Balad. He explains that the invasion in 2003 was short and quick because our military bypassed major cities to get to Baghdad and topple the government. In 2004, the mission changed to clearing the villages and towns; that task was continuing at the time of this interview.

Brumfield was battalion chaplain, which meant that he went on missions with his team. Before every mission, he would announce, "I'm going to have prayer. If you would like to join me, I will be here at my Humvee." He found the soldiers anxious to participate. "We would gather in a circle, lock arms, and pray for safety. Upon arrival at our destination or completion of our campaign, we would again pause to offer thanks."

As a noncombatant, Brumfield did not carry a weapon but reports that he had great confidence in the individuals with whom he served—both officers and enlisted. He explains, "I felt as safe as one could under the circumstances. I was part of several convoys that were attacked by the enemy. Sometimes roadside bombs hit us. At other times, after being stopped by a bomb, we were ambushed and forced into a firefight. A couple of times, we came close to not coming back. I just knew that it was the Lord; God's people back home were praying. Our unit lost thirty-eight men, and countless others were injured."

The chaplain points out that radical Muslims butchered over forty Iraqi soldiers assigned to his post, simply because the new army had trained them. He says friendly Iraqis never know who is or is not hostile. "They live in fear and therefore will not express their opposition to radical elements in their country."

Once, when leaving the mess hall, Brumfield and five of his teammates were talking with a captain from another unit. "If we had talked thirty seconds longer," he marvels, "we would all have been killed. As we crossed the compound, a mortar exploded directly behind us. We jumped into a hole and waited for an opportunity to run to a nearby medical building. Two airmen who narrowly escaped the blast met us there. After a time of rejoicing, we, along with medical personnel already in the building, joined in a prayer of thanksgiving. On my last mission before leaving Iraq, my team apprehended two terrorists as they were placing a bomb on the side of the road. I think lives were spared because of our interception."

According to Brumfield, his job was not strictly religious. One of his responsibilities was to educate soldiers on correct protocol when interacting with the Iraqi people. For instance, in meetings with the Iraqi, seating should be according to rank. The sheik is always seated at the head of the table and must be served first. To ask him to "help himself" is disrespectful to him and thus to the entire tribe. Also, to sit with legs crossed in the presence of Iraqis, showing the bottom of the shoe, is to imply an attempt to subvert them—put them under the foot. Another cultural difference involves approaching the door of an Iraqi home; a caller should stand to the side after knocking, lest the inside of the home become visible. This allows the resident to determine who can see into or enter his or her home. "Insensitivity to these issues creates a barrier and hinders the ability of the military to work with the Iraqi people."

Another of Brumfield's duties as chaplain was to provide counseling. "Drugs and alcohol are readily available in Iraq. Both are forbidden in a combat zone—off-base as well as on—but sometimes rules are broken and intervention is required," he notes. "As could be expected, soldiers worry about families back home, how they are coping with added responsibilities and altered lifestyles. Female soldiers, forced to leave children with relatives or friends, miss having greater input into the growth and development of their offspring. Occasionally, enlisted personnel will have issues with commanding officers and need to talk about them with an objective person they have come to trust."

One of the most somber occasions for a chaplain occurs when a member of his unit is killed. "It is especially hard on those who were close friends with the victim or were present when it happened," recalls the clergyman. Having gotten to know all members of his team through close proximity and shared missions, Brumfield identified with their grief and was in a good position to provide ministry. He also conducted memorial services that were attended by everyone from the division commander down. This gave all involved an opportunity to pay honor and respect to fallen comrades. Chaplains in the United States are called upon to provide support for families of the deceased, although letters of condolence and information regarding memorial services are sent from the field.

Brumfield confides that, as a minister, his greatest experiences centered on seeing people come to know Christ. He personally led seventy-seven soldiers to salvation. Most responded as a result of one-on-one contact rather than during invitation at the close of a formal service. He baptized forty-four, with others choosing to wait and be baptized in their home churches. "We built a camouflage baptismal with sandbag steps," he says, smiling. "One baptism service drew a crowd of three hundred. We had a praise band composed of musically gifted GIs. Those who observed cheered as each candidate came out of the water. Later, service people who wanted to rededicate their lives to Christ knelt around the baptismal and placed their hands in the water as an indication of their renewed commitment."

Brumfield insists that many Iraqi villagers support the presence of American forces. Others resent foreigners being in their country. Surprisingly, many Muslims are respectful of Christian chaplains, calling them "men of the Book." Some imams enjoy engaging chaplains in conversation about their divergent beliefs; others oppose such discussions. Sometimes Muslims accompany soldiers to services, basking in the open, accepting atmosphere. Also, there is a small minority of Iraqi Christians—called Caledonian Christians—who relish attending spiritual meetings.

When Brumfield left Iraq, he went to Fort Bragg. He was delighted to be stationed so close to home. On Valentine's Day, February 14, 2005, he received his final discharge. Asked his impression of today's military, he states emphatically, "I found them to be good, hardworking, patriotic, young people, devoted to doing a good job and representing America well."

Dick Cartwright

The most aggravating job I ever had was guarding
inmates from the prison camp at Fort Meade.

66 **T**here was nothing going on in 1960–1961," asserts
Dick Cartwright. "I never got off the East Coast." The
Madison native served eighteen months in the US Army
before receiving a hardship discharge, due to his father's sudden heart
attack. Cartwright, an only son, came home to manage the family
business.

After volunteering for the draft on March 22, 1960, the young recruit
underwent basic training at Fort Jackson, South Carolina, on Tank Hill.
From there, he traveled to Fort Gordon, Georgia, where he operated the
telephone switchboard for three months.

Cartwright's next stop was Fort Meade, Maryland, his home for the
majority of his time in uniform. While there, he was part of a strategic
force trained to provide support to other units within twenty-four hours
after notification. But when the Cuban Missile Crisis arose, he was rushed
to Eglin, Florida, to help supply telephone support for the approximately
ten thousand troops standing by on alert. He remained there for six to eight
weeks. After successful resolution of that situation, Cartwright returned
to Fort Meade—a week's journey by convoy—with overnight stops in
Fort Bragg and Fort Benning, Georgia. When he reached Maryland, he
became attached to the Sixty-Ninth Signal Corps, Company B.

"The most aggravating job I ever had," he contends, "was guarding
inmates from the prison camp at Fort Meade. These were not serious

criminals, mostly kids committing minor infractions, such as going AWOL." Each guard was in charge of two prisoners. "We were not allowed to fire our weapons or use a stick, but if we failed to report an incident, or if one escaped, we could get busted." In the winter, prisoners cleared snow while guards stood watch. "Sometimes we would get so cold, we would let them hold our weapons while we shoveled snow."

With help from the American Red Cross, Cartwright was discharged on October 4, 1961. He was required to serve four additional years in the Army Reserves, but since there was no reserve unit in Rockingham County at that time, he did not have to attend meetings on a regular basis. He would, however, spend two weeks each year filing papers for the Third Army Headquarters in Atlanta, Georgia.

Upon his return, Cartwright commenced working at the only job he ever held—operating Dick's GI, a retail business known as the Army and Navy Store, before learning that private companies were not allowed to use that title. The name of the business was later changed to Dick's Store, after Wrangler refused to sell jeans to them, believing them to be a discount warehouse similar to the once-popular GI 1200 stores.

Cartwright married the former Evelyn Harrell of Oak Ridge. The couple has three children: Steven Edwards, Stephanie Nelson, and Christie Fox. Fox currently manages the multigenerational enterprise, which, five years ago, became M. R. Promotions.

William H. "Pansy" Collins

I'm not any better than those soldier boys.

I never met Pansy Collins. The first time I heard his name, a friend was describing his funeral service. Right away, I regretted not having known him. Assigned to a medical unit during World War II, one of Collins's responsibilities was to go onto the field of battle and collect the dead and wounded, whom he would then transport to a makeshift hospital. Collins never got over the emotional impact of plucking mangled young bodies from the ravages of war and depositing them not in the sterile environment of a well-equipped ambulance, but on the back of a rugged, uncomfortable, three-quarter-ton military vehicle.

Lamenting to his wife, "I'm not any better than those soldier boys," Collins requested that at his death he be carried to the church in the back of a pickup truck in their memory. He also asked to be buried in a body bag, but after understandable objection from family members, he agreed to a pine coffin. When the time came, in August 2006, his truck was draped with the American flag. His son drove, and his grandsons rode in the back with the body as they made their way from the funeral home to the church.

Collins, a lifelong resident of Rockingham County, dropped out of high school at age sixteen to help support his family. He worked at Washington Mills in Mayodan and also for the state, repairing roads. In 1939, at the suggestion of his family doctor, he enlisted in the National Guard. He had been a member just a few weeks when he was called up for active duty. He served in the Thirtieth Infantry, a medical field-hospital unit.

Collins went to Fort Jackson, South Carolina, for five months; there he practiced setting up and moving hospitals and treating mock patients. He did the same thing in Tennessee and along the North Carolina–South Carolina border. In the swamps near Camp Blanding, Florida, he learned to carry out operations in water and sand. After a short stint at Camp Atterbury, Indiana, he went to Boston, Massachusetts, where he boarded the USS *LeJeune* to sail to England. He arrived in Chichester in 1942 to train for the invasion of Omaha Beach, scheduled June 6, 1944 (D-day).

In May, his unit relocated near the English Channel. They watched the buildup of equipment on the Cliffs of Dover. Four days prior to D-day, they were confined to the area with instructions to remain silent. "Loose lips sink ships" became the mantra. The men practiced camouflaging their vehicles with nets and hiding them under trees and underbrush.

Collins, en route to Omaha Beach on June 10—D-day plus four—had entered the waters in a small LST. Other vessels, massive and moderate, filled the channel. Suddenly, the weather grew turbulent; smaller crafts were ordered back to shore. Collins remembers being disappointed: "After all the training, I was ready to see some action."

Finally, on June 12, six days after D-day, he got his wish. He crossed the channel in the same LST and pushed his way onto Omaha Beach. After a relatively uneventful landing, he deftly maneuvered his truck— which had been modified to allow movement in water—up the hill for reassembly. In the distance, he could hear machine gun fire, the deafening sounds of heavy bombardment.

"Corporal Collins, what is *that*?" inquired a bewildered Kentucky youth.

"Son," Collins replied, "*that* is the war."

The soldiers set up their hospital while German planes circled overhead, attempting to halt Allied advances by wiping out supplies and equipment. Collins drove his truck back and forth, picking up medical goods from the supply depot and hauling water from the water tank. "Wounded men began arriving before we were ready," he says. "At first, we flew them to England. Later, we functioned as a first aid hospital, patching patients up and getting them to evacuee hospitals." The unit moved up about every two weeks, tearing down and setting up equipment each time they relocated. Plodding forward in this manner, they made their way through France, Belgium, and Holland.

Collins was in Belgium during the Battle of the Bulge. Occurring between December 16, 1944, and January 25, 1945, this was the biggest and bloodiest battle American forces faced during World War II. More than eighty-nine thousand men were killed, wounded, captured, or missing. Collins, assigned to the motor pool, was often called upon to go to the front line to pick up fallen soldiers. He was always surprised to be fired on, despite Red Cross markings showing on his helmet and shoulders.

After the Battle of the Bulge, "the war went from bad to worse for the Germans," recalls Collins. "They were short on food, short on supplies, and short on morale." He describes driving down the road and seeing two German soldiers standing in an open field holding a white flag. He waved them over and discovered that the entire company of one hundred men wanted to surrender. "I motioned for them to follow me and led them down the road to the stockade—quite a coup for a corporal!" Allied forces hopscotched across Germany until the armies of Nazi Germany officially surrendered on May 8, 1945—VE Day (Pansy Collins. Interview. June 6, 2006).

In November 1945, after forty-two months of active service, Collins was discharged from the military. He came home to Madison and "loafed around for a while." After short stints with a trucking outfit and a grocery store, he went to work for Lee Telephone Company, his employment home for the next fifty years. In 1950, he married the former Polly Stanfield, who continues to live in the house Collins built for her. The couple has two children, four grandchildren, and five great-grandchildren. He remained active in veterans' affairs until his death.

William H. "Pansy" Collins died August 18, 2006.

Henry Lee "Pete" Comer

They all wore identifying numbers on cords around their
necks, because that's the way their victims were identified.

O n July 13, 1945, at around 5:30 in the afternoon, eighteen-
year-old Henry Lee "Pete" Comer of Stoneville left Fort
Bragg on an Army troop train headed for—he wasn't sure.
He recalls being occupied with one thought: for most of his life, he
had experienced periodic, debilitating headaches. They came upon
him without warning, leaving him nauseated, unable to function, and
often blind, sometimes for as long as ten hours. "Always, in the back
of my mind," he says, "I was afraid I would be hit with this terrible
pain." Fortunately, migraines—as they came to be known—did not
prevent Comer from photographing the trial of one of the most heinous
atrocities perpetrated against American troops in Europe during World
War II, nor did they prevent him from discovering his life's work.

Comer learned that he was going to Camp Robertson, Arkansas.
At around 8:30 p.m., the train pulled into the little town of Hamlet,
where appreciative townspeople boarded the train and passed out
peaches. After that tasty interlude, the train chugged its way through
Georgia, Alabama, and Tennessee. When they reached Nashville, Comer
remembers thinking, "I'd really rather be going to the Grand Ole Opry."
Finally they arrived in Arkansas, where the inductees spent seventeen
weeks in basic training. Comer worked in the kitchen for a while.

On December 15, 1945, he was ordered to report to Camp Pickett,
Virginia. Since it was so close to Christmas, he requested, and was

ultimately granted, three additional days. Eventually, Comer made it to Camp Pickett. While there, he joined the regular army, thus earning a $200 bonus and a thirty-day leave. After the leave, Comer spent approximately two weeks each in Fort Bragg, Camp Pickett, and Camp Kilmer, New Jersey, before boarding the *George Washington* to sail for Europe. "I believe those delays placed me in Germany at the exact time men were needed for the signal corps," he explains. "I have always believed that there was a special hand at play."

The ship docked in Le Havre, France, on the fifteenth of March— Comer's birthday. It was here he received his first impression of war. "The area had been bombed to pieces by the Allies on D-day. All I saw were miles of flattened devastation. Once in a while, I would see a rider on a bike or three-wheeler, but no other signs of life. Metal remains of ships jutted out of the harbor." From here, tractors and trailers carried the men to Camp Phillip Morris, where they spent one night sleeping on the floor in cold tents. "The next morning, we were fed pancakes; I was so hungry, I went through the line twice," admits Comer, who watched in amazement as Frenchmen fought over food from garbage cans. "I will never forget that," he adds.

On the evening of July 17, the men were loaded into French railroad cars called forty-and-eights. During World War I, these thirteen-ton boxcars were used to transport forty men and eight horses; on this day, however, Comer was one of only twenty-five men—no horses. There was no heat in the cars, and again the GIs slept on the floor. Three days later, they arrived at the Replacement Center in Marburg, Germany. "I had a sore throat and high fever, so I had to report to the medic. When I got back, I found out that I had been assigned PX duty, unloading two-and-a-half-ton coal trucks."

Two days later, Comer was one of eighty men selected to go to Wiesbaden, Germany, to a signal corps outfit. This was his introduction to photography. "When I was interviewed to determine whether I would like to work in still photography or motion pictures, I chose movies because I had operated the projector in my local movie house.

"During training," declares Comer, "I was sent to a nearby town to make photographs. As I came to the middle of town, I saw several shepherds traveling together with their sheep. I wondered how in the world they would separate those sheep after they had been watered. But each shepherd just called his sheep by name, and they followed him. I thought of what Jesus said in John 10:4: 'the sheep follow Him: for they know His voice.'"

Comer's first assignment was to go to Bremerhaven to photograph the arrival of the *Thomas Barry*—the ship bringing the first American dependents to visit their husbands and fathers. Comer photographed most of the families as they disembarked. "I went aboard ship to photograph the wife of General Mark Clark," he emphasizes. But his most memorable assignment occurred when he was tapped to film the Malmedy Massacre Trial, which took place at the War Crimes Building in Dachau, Germany, from May to June 1946. Two cameras were involved: one was equipped with sound; the other—Comer's—was not. While there, he stayed in quarters previously occupied by German troops.

"Malmedy Massacre" refers to the execution of unarmed American prisoners of war by members of the First Panzer Division, a German combat unit under the command of Lieutenant Colonel Jochen Peiper, on December 17, 1944—the second day of the Battle of the Bulge. The Americans, members of the 285th Field Artillery Observation Battalion, were herded into an open field on the outskirts of Malmedy, Belgium. According to eyewitness accounts, there were about 120 men in the clearing. For reasons no one understands, the Germans suddenly opened fire on the prisoners with machine guns.

Before the German soldiers left the area, they shot, at close range, any American who showed signs of life. Even so, a few managed to save themselves by feigning death. Some prisoners escaped and tried to hide in a nearby café. German soldiers set fire to the café and shot anyone attempting to escape the flames. Eventually, forty-three survivors made it to Allied lines.

On January 14, 1945, four weeks after the slaughter, seventy-two bodies were removed from the field; they had been buried in two feet of snow. Four months later, another twelve bodies were discovered lying further away. This brought the total number of victims to eighty-four ("Malmedy Massacre").

Through the lens of his camera, Comer could see clearly the more than seventy defendants. He describes the scene: "They all wore identifying numbers on cords around their necks, because that's the way their victims had to be identified. There was Private First Class Georg Fleps, former soldier in the Schutzstaffel (SS). He was pointed out by one of the witnesses as the person who fired the first two shots. An American soldier held up his hands to demonstrate how he tried to surrender. Other survivors told how the Nazis laughed as they moved about the field, shooting or bashing with a rifle butt anyone who moved."

Comer listened and filmed as Trial Judge Advocate, Lieutenant Colonel Burton F. Ellis, argued the case against the Schutzstaffel soldiers and as Lieutenant Colonel Willis M. Everett presented the defense. "All the defendants were found guilty after only two hours and twenty minutes of deliberation by the panel of judges: forty-two men were sentenced to death by hanging; twenty-two to life in prison; the rest received either ten, fifteen, or twenty-year prison terms." Comer recalls thinking, "If I had been born in Germany, I could have been one of those guys sitting over there." The forty-three death sentences were later commuted to prison sentences, and by 1956, *all* of the men had been released.

After the trial, Comer worked for a while at the photography lab in Munich; this brought him in close proximity to the famous and infamous: "In 1946, I photographed five-star general Dwight D. Eisenhower, Army Chief of Staff, from a distance of about four feet. I also visited the home of Joseph Goebbels' mother. Goebbels was Adolph Hitler's minister of propaganda, who poisoned his six children and had an aide shoot him and his wife after Germany fell. I met his brother—a film director in California—but I was not allowed to meet or photograph Mrs. Goebbels. Her son said that she had already been through enough."

Comer visited the Dachau Concentration Camp, established in March 1933, on the grounds of an abandoned munitions factory—the first regular concentration camp established by the Nazi party. The camp was divided into sections—the camp area and the crematoria. The courtyard was used for summary execution of prisoners. An electric barbed wire fence, a ditch, and a wall with seven guard towers surrounded the camp.

In all, 238,000 prisoners, from thirty countries, were housed at Dachau. In addition to the executions, hundreds died or were permanently disabled from medical experimentation. The exact number of those who died will probably never be known. American forces liberated the prisoners held there in April 1945. "Even today, I cannot talk about my visit to that chamber of death without choking back tears," acknowledges Comer.

After eighteen and one-half months' active duty, Comer returned to his hometown. He married Jackie Roberts of Madison, to whom he has been married for sixty-five years as of this writing. They have one daughter, Carolyn Lee Price, and two grandchildren, Brandon and Lisa Beth.

In 1948, Comer went to Kansas Photography School on the GI Bill to obtain additional training, and the rest, as they say, is history. Comers Photography is known and respected throughout the local and surrounding areas. He has traveled to Virginia, Georgia, and Indiana, to photograph special occasions. His photography has won first place in North Carolina competitions, and his work has been recognized nationally.

Robert "Bob" Comer

I was there when Chinese Nationals were evacuated from Mainland China—through Guam—to Taiwan.

Join the Marines and see the world. And if that is not enough, join the Air Force and see some more. At least, that formula worked for Bob Comer of Stoneville, who entered the Marine Corps on January 6, 1948, and exited on June 19, 1956. One year later, he entered the Air Force, where he served until August 1, 1969, at which time he celebrated his second and final retirement from military service.

By the time Comer took his basic training at Parris Island, South Carolina, World War II had come to an end. He spent four months in Pearl Harbor learning to be a supply administrator before being sent to Guam—scene of one of the great battles of the Pacific War. The United States retained a postwar presence on the island. "We were there to clean up debris left from battle and to ship supplies back to the states," Comer says. He was engaged in this effort from August 1948 until October 1949. Most of the used equipment was sold to China. "I was there when Chinese Nationals were evacuated from Mainland China—through Guam—to Taiwan," he adds.

Next, Comer went to Barstow Marine Base in California and from there to Camp Pendleton, to undergo combat training in preparation for deployment to Korea. He was in Korea from November 1951 until November 1952. "All supplies for the Korean War came out of the Army budget," he explains. "My job was to serve as liaison between the Army and the First Marine Division, making sure that the Marines received all the materials to which they were entitled."

Comer describes living conditions in the war zone as bleak: "I lived in a crowded tent with three other Marines. There were no showers, so we flattened out a helmet and warmed enough water on a gas stove to wash our faces and brush our teeth." Once, as a Christmas treat, the men were promised a hot shower. A Steam Jenny was rigged to draw water from the river and heat it. "The contraption made a couple of loud groans and died," frets Comer. The disappointed men waited five additional months before enjoying their Yuletide showers.

The 1951 winter and spring campaigns, as well as the 1952 winter offensive, occurred while Comer was in Korea. Yet the closest he came to being injured was from friendly fire. He tells of one such incident: "We heard incoming artillery and hit the ground. Later, we found out that an American battalion, preparing to return to the front line, was going through training exercises—firing at a mountain." Unexpectedly, some of their projectiles came over the peak and landed dangerously near fellow Marines. Fortunately, no one was hurt. Comer was promoted to buck sergeant in 1951 and staff sergeant in 1952.

"The Korean people were starving," states Comer matter-of-factly. He recalls traveling to Seoul in a three-truck convoy, delivering spare parts to a relocation point. Great gusts of snow pelted the windshields of their vehicles, making it hard for them to see the road. They decided to stop for a smoke. Suddenly, a Korean child—they judged him to be about two to three years of age—seemed to materialize from nowhere. He was just standing there in the snow naked.

"Chop! Chop!" called the boy.

"We better get out of here," cautioned Comer. "If that kid is here, somebody *else* is here." The men thrust a can of C-rations into the waif's hand and hurried away, leaving him shivering by the side of the road.

In Seoul, the Army maintained a compound for military personnel passing through the area. A chain-link fence surrounded the mess hall.

Barrels of hot water were provided for cleaning mess kits after meals. Outside the fence, hungry locals routinely gathered.

"Chop! Chop!" they pled.

Benevolent Marines slapped their mess kits against the fence before dipping them into the water; grateful Koreans picked up the leftover food that passed through the wire and landed on the ground. "To them it was a welcome treat," assures Comer.

Comer left Korea in 1952 and arrived at Camp Lejeune. He requested assignment to recruiter school and was accepted. Before he could begin, however, a captain with whom he had served in Korea asked that the sergeant be transferred to his outfit. The only way that could happen was for Comer to be reassigned to supply and administration, complete that training, and then join the officer in Albany, Georgia—which he did. "I was there until 1956, when I left the Marine Corps," he says.

For the next year, Comer worked with Wesson Oil Products–Blue Plate Division, while continuing to live in Albany. Even so, it was not long before he became dissatisfied with civilian life. He drove across town to Turner Air Force Base and enlisted in the Air Force. He retained the rank he had earned in the Marines and was once again assigned to supply and administration. From June through December 1958, he relocated to Germany and Italy on a NATO support operation with the Thirty-Eighth Fighter Squadron. He was in charge of flyaway kits—twenty-two metal bins holding spare parts to support fighter squadrons deployed overseas.

Afterward, he returned to his home base in Albany; he was there until 1961, when he was assigned to a Field Activity Group out of Washington, DC, and sent to Fairbanks, Alaska, to work on a top-secret government project. "I can't tell you anything about that, except that I worked around the clock. In the twenty-two months I was there, I took only two days' leave." Obviously, the twenty-four hour days and nights did not concern him.

In April 1963, Comer was transferred to the historic city of Toledo, Spain. He was attached to the same project as in Alaska but did not have to work as many hours. In September, he sent for Joanne Turner, a civilian coworker from Denver, Colorado, whom he had met while she was working with the Department of Defense at the University of Denver. She and her dog flew to Spain, where the couple wed in both a civil ceremony in Madrid and a more formal one at the Air Base. They developed a warm relationship with the Spanish people, enjoying the beauty and culture of the region. They returned to Pope Air Force Base in September 1966.

Comer volunteered to go to Southeast Asia in 1967. He was stationed at Korat Air Force Base in Thailand until February 15, 1968. When he left there, he went to Hollomon Air Force Base in Alameda, New Mexico, and stayed there until his retirement. He was already home in Rockingham County when he was notified that he was being awarded the Air Force Accommodation Award for outstanding service beyond the call of duty. He was invited to travel to Pope Air Force Base for formal presentation but chose instead to have it mailed to his home.

For ten years, Comer simultaneously farmed and ran a service garage housed on his property. He then worked twelve years with locally owned Macfield, Inc., a yarn texturing company, before retiring from civilian employment. He has three children—sons Robert and Barry and daughter Michelle Lester, who was born in Spain, weighing in at a mere three pounds and four ounces.

Regrettably, Comer's wife passed away in 1990. In 2001, he married Eunice Shelton; "Eunice keeps me on track," he reports.

Ken Crowder

*I never felt that I was going to die. I determined
that whatever happened, I would accept it.*

en Crowder faced his greatest challenge some forty-eight years *after* leaving military service. On the morning of January 29, 2005, he went to his barn to feed the cows. On the way back, he noticed that his "arms felt like they were going to sleep." Later, he and Barbara, his wife, went to Madison to run errands, and he again mentioned that his arms "felt funny." The couple returned home, and Crowder sat down at his computer. His wife brought him a glass of tea, thinking that would make him feel better. He could not lift the glass. His arms would not move. Barbara called the doctor and was told to get her husband to the hospital immediately.

Crowder walked into Reidsville's Annie Penn Hospital unassisted but stated that he needed to use the restroom while waiting for help. He soon came back and complained that he couldn't unbutton his pants. Barbara noticed a strange look in his eyes and pointed that out to the attending physician. Crowder was taken to a back room and given a shot. A nurse started to work with him immediately. After an initial call to Cone Hospital in Greensboro, the decision was made to take Crowder to North Carolina Baptist Hospital in Winston-Salem. It was snowing steadily, so Barbara was allowed to ride in the ambulance rather than follow alone in her car. "Strap my arms down so they won't fall," requested Crowder.

They arrived in the Baptist emergency room at about five o'clock in the afternoon and waited there all night. At eight o'clock the next morning, a bed became available. Crowder was diagnosed with stroke of the spine. Barbara remembers doctors with opposing views discussing whether or not to operate. They waited. On February 7, surgery was performed on Crowder's neck to make room for his swollen spinal cord. He began to get feeling in his legs and feet.

After about a week in the hospital, Crowder was transferred to the Baptist Hospital Stitch Center, where he received therapy twice daily. At that point, he could neither stand nor walk. Two therapists held him on the exercise equipment. This continued until March 10, when he was allowed to return home. For several weeks, a home health therapist came to the house daily. This was reduced to three times per week during March and April. Afterward, Crowder was carried to a rehabilitation center in Eden for treatment.

In June, Crowder began to experience problems with his back and returned to the hospital for surgery designed to allow movement in his legs. Apparently, his sciatic nerve had been affected. He was in the hospital seven or eight days before he began to improve. Once home, he was assigned a health nurse to assist with bathing and walking.

Today, Crowder walks without support, a feat that amazes even his doctors. He does not have full use of his hands, although he can perform some tasks. The stroke, uncharacteristically, did not damage his heart or lungs. Crowder gets frustrated at times because he can't do what he always did, but he never questions God. "I never felt that I was going to die," he declares. "I determined that whatever happened, I would accept it."

I ask about his military career. "I volunteered for the Marine Corps on May 31, 1957, to get out of the tobacco field," he begins. "For basic training, I was sent to Parris Island, South Carolina, where just one year earlier, Recruit Platoon 71 was ordered to perform a nighttime disciplinary march into the marshes of Ribbon Creek, and six recruits drowned. In my barracks, the back door was right over that swamp, but reforms and guidelines had been instituted, so that by the time I got there, a person in good physical condition was able to complete the sixteen weeks without major difficulty." Because of previous National Guard involvement, Crowder began his career as a private first class, making him the "highest paid boot in the company."

Next, Crowder went to Camp Geiger, located at Camp Lejeune, for four weeks of advanced infantry training. There he was assigned to the Second Marine Division Headquarters and Service Company. Because he had taken business courses in high school, he was given administrative duties. "I loved being battalion mail clerk," he says. "I went into the fields where troops were performing training exercises and set up post offices. My transportation was a helicopter that resembled an eggbeater, thanks to two props protruding from the top. I picked up mail in bags, sorted it, and then delivered it to the men."

From Camp Geiger, Crowder went to Vegas, Puerto Rico, for ninety days of war games. "We sailed there on an old merchant ship that was consigned to the military," he recalls. "For seven days, I tried to sleep in a deck hammock, while it swayed back and forth, back and forth. I got so seasick; I developed a lifelong preference for land." Once he reached the island, however, he enjoyed the beautiful oceans and balmy temperatures as he performed mail duties and mimeographed copies of personnel files.

Crowder was transferred to G-1 section, Fleet Marine Force, Atlantic, at Camp Elmore Marine Headquarters in Norfolk Naval Base. There his duties included keeping a roster of available personnel and supplying names for transfer to various camps upon request. "When I had free time, I enjoyed playing basketball in the gymnasium," he explains. "During a scrimmage game, I jumped for a ball. As I came down, another player bumped into me and knocked me to the floor. I landed on my wrists— breaking both of them." Unable to perform his duties with both arms in a cast, Crowder was sent to Portsmouth Naval Hospital to recuperate. He never returned to administrative duty.

Crowder's father, a farmer who also served as assistant jailer, had undergone surgery for colon cancer. Needing help to care for his tobacco crop, he applied for a hardship discharge for the oldest of his seven children. Although he was enjoying life as a Marine, Crowder came home to Madison to work in the tobacco field. Later, Fieldcrest Mills in Eden employed him. It was there he met Barbara Leffew, who worked in the general office. The couple married on October 3, 1959. They have one son, two grandchildren, and one great-grandchild. Besides commercially subcontracting homes, Crowder has, at various times, been associated with both Dupont and Leffew Construction Company. He eventually returned to full-time farming.

Today, five years after Crowder's stroke, he and Barbara continue to live on the family farm. An avid Bible scholar, he teaches Sunday School at Stone-Eden Baptist Church.

Laura Mae DuFore

Remembered as America's Second-Oldest Female Veteran

At seventeen, with no money and a ninth-grade education, Laura Mae DuFore fled the harsh life of her family farm and north Michigan lumber camps to make it on her own. She never looked back—waiting tables and working in knitting mills, factories, and hospitals to supply her needs. She saved enough money to enroll in the Marinello School of Beauty, earned a diploma in cosmetology, and found employment as a beauty operator—pocketing a grand total of seven dollars each week. She supplemented her income by styling hair and applying makeup for female corpses in a local mortuary. Through hard work and careful money management, she was able, in time, to purchase her own shop and eventually hire additional help.

The feisty entrepreneur married once. As she explains in her autobiography, *A Life So Full*, her husband refused to work, so she gave him a year to get his act together. When he refused, she kicked him out.

Like all Americans, DuFore was troubled when she heard of the Japanese attack on Pearl Harbor. One day, she left her establishment to go downtown and shop. Instead, she found herself at the enlistment office, where she joined the Women's Auxiliary Corps (WAC), a brand new organization. At thirty-nine, she narrowly missed the cutoff age for enlistment, which was forty. She was transported to Chicago and introduced to a group of fellow enlistees; together they traveled to Oglethorpe, Georgia, for basic training. There they found chaos: no uniforms, untrained officers, and bad food. On top of that, many of them were quite ill from a series of injections.

After six hard weeks at Oglethorpe, DuFore was transferred to Stockton Field, California, where she enjoyed a totally different experience, finding her new quarters comfortable and the food delicious. She was assigned to the message center, but before long, an order came in for an O67-clerk, non-typist. That was DuFore. The next two weeks found her back at Oglethorpe enduring more shots and training; then in Pittsburg, California, for much the same—plus uniforms; and finally in San Francisco, boarding the USS *Monterrey* to sail for Dutch New Guinea. From there she moved into a war zone—Hollandia.

There was no supply area in Hollandia, just jungle. The women could not take showers, even though blue dye from their life preservers had rubbed off on their skin and clothing. Pants had to be borrowed from GIs and tied on with GI belts. The girls slept six to a tent, under mosquito netting. DuFore heard there was a hospital nearby and gained permission to volunteer her services: she lit cigarettes, listened, fluffed pillows, listened, held distraught patients, listened, wrote letters, and listened. Since no one was allowed to know where the men were, their return address read simply "Somewhere in New Guinea."

The WACs left Hollandia for Leyte (in the Philippines) a few months after Christmas, 1944, at 2:00 a.m., in an overcrowded airplane with a girlie picture painted on the side. They had to keep shifting positions to maintain altitude. When they landed, they encountered devastation as far as their eyes could see. They found their tents in crude piles, full of rotting holes. The only existing structures were a mess tent and a latrine. Foxholes were filled with water. Before retiring, the exhausted women had to raise tents and dig new foxholes, tasks made more difficult by frequent alerts of incoming artillery, forcing them to abandon their chores and seek shelter. WACs assumed responsibility for clerical duties as soon as possible, freeing male soldiers to join the battle.

When DuFore left Leyte, she was stationed a few miles outside of Manila, capital city of the Philippines. Parts of the city were still burning when she arrived; most everything else had been leveled. She put perfume in her nostrils to tolerate the stench from decaying bodies still buried in the rubble. Japanese soldiers remained hidden in walled areas. While there, DuFore toured what had been a teaching hospital. On the top floor she saw remains of prisoners who had been tortured or shot and left to die. She was still in the Philippines on August 15, 1945, when Japan surrendered, following atomic bomb attacks on Hiroshima and Nagasaki.

When the war ended, DuFore returned to Michigan. Unable to find what she wanted there, she moved to California and purchased both a beauty shop and a home. Always open to new opportunities, she obtained her real estate license and, for a time, pursued both careers. She eventually became a successful real estate speculator. She was also a gifted artist and avid gardener. Her boundless energy and business acumen allowed her to travel extensively: the Orient, Australia, New Zealand, and Hawaii.

In 1995, DuFore moved to eastern North Carolina. In 2005, at age 101, she completed her autobiography, which she sold—along with her paintings—at the Farmer's Market in New Bern, to help pay her expenses. On August 30, 2007, at 103, after a long and eventful life, Laura Mae DuFore died quietly at a veterans' rest home in Fayetteville (DuFore, *A Life So Full*).

Clyde Easter Jr.

I'm glad I served; I did what I thought was right for my country.

C lyde Easter was in Fort Hood, Texas, in October 1962, when the Cuban Missile Crisis occurred. His unit was loaded onto a troop train and carried to Fort Stewart, Georgia, where they were quarantined for weeks. They were not told where they were, nor were they permitted to make telephone calls or write letters. Eventually, they traveled by convoy to Fort Lauderdale, Florida, still unaware of their mission. From there, they sailed to the coast of Cuba on what they surmised to be a routine training exercise. Instead, they were held aboard ship indefinitely, ready to respond to any hostile reaction from the Russians.

Easter had joined the Marine National Guard in May 1955. After participating in summer camp in 1957, however, he opted to discontinue attending meetings. He was drafted into the Army on November 28, 1961, and completed basic training at Fort Jackson, South Carolina, February 9, 1962. From that location, he was transferred to Fort Hood.

After peaceful resolution of the Cuban Missile Crisis, Easter, an E-4, returned to Fort Hood, where he remained for the duration of his tenure. Assigned to communications, he was in charge of operating the telephone switchboard. When his unit went into the field for practice maneuvers, he took incoming calls and forwarded them to the appropriate personnel.

Easter was discharged on May 5, 1964. Returning to Rockingham County, he found it difficult to locate employment. "I'd looked all over," he says. "Many people were not positive toward the military at that time.

Vietnam veterans were stereotyped, but I'm *glad* I served," he states emphatically. "I did what I thought was right for my country." He finally found work with Lee Telephone Company, first in Martinsville, Virginia, and then in Madison.

Easter and his wife, Delores, have one son, Clyde Easter III.

Bill Freeman

I get upset when I think about Vietnam veterans
coming home to be called names or spat on. People
have no idea what those guys went through.

Young Bill Freeman loved the military. He always wanted to wear a uniform and serve his country. He spoke of his dream with two uncles: one a soldier, the other a Marine. Each agreed to tell him *one* war story. The World War II veterans proceeded to detail their most horrifying experiences on the battlefield, the Marine emphasizing that he had undergone treatment for shell-shock after being compelled to slip up behind an enemy guard and strangle him with a piano wire while capturing an oil depot. Each man concluded his tale with a stern warning.

"Son, don't *ever* join the Army," warned the soldier.

"*Never* become a Marine," added the Marine.

Since Freeman disliked the look of the Navy uniform, he turned his attention to the Air Force. He graduated from Madison-Mayodan High School on June 2, 1962, and twelve days later reported to Lackland Air Force Base just outside the city limits of San Antonio, Texas, for basic training. From there, he went to Sheppard Air Force Base in Wichita Falls, Texas, to learn to be a jet engine mechanic. He was eventually stationed at Columbus Air Force Base in Mississippi, Second Air Force Strategic Air Command (SAC), 454 Bomb Wing.

Freeman says that during the time he was in Mississippi, due to the instability of relations with Russia, America kept four B-52 bombers armed with atomic warheads in the air at all times. They were refueled by KC-135s—the first jet-powered aerial refueling tankers in the United States Air Force—also housed and maintained at Columbus. The bombers carried top-secret orders in sealed envelopes, awaiting a signal from the Pentagon to open and proceed toward specified targets.

Freeman's unit was sent to Guam to fly bombing missions into Vietnam. His job was to keep the aircraft in good working order. While the pilots were on bombing raids, which usually took eight to twelve hours, he and the other mechanics serviced planes on the ground. When the fliers returned, their crafts were examined for needed repair; fuel and oil were replenished, and sheet metal specialists patched up damages incurred from ground-to-air missiles. Freeman put in a request to become a door gunner. "I wanted to be a part of the action, but when I found out that life expectancy in that position was about thirty seconds, I was kind of glad I didn't get it.

"Our outfit flew one hundred missions without losing an airplane," declares Freeman with obvious pride. He points out that it was not unusual for bombardiers to release more than seven hundred bombs on one airdrop. "They would open the bomb bay doors, and all I could see were bombs dropping out. Our B-52s made that place look like the moon, there were so many craters.

"Sometimes American troops, pinned down by North Vietnamese, would call in their coordinates and request that our pilots strafe or bomb the enemy to allow them to escape. Some never made it out." Freeman interrupts his narrative to share a deep felt emotion: "I get upset when I think about Vietnam veterans coming home to be called names or spat on. People have no idea what those guys went through. Every step they took in that jungle could have resulted in serious injury or death."

The Guamanians welcomed the Americans to their island. "They were glad we were there," remembers Freeman. "They planned a luau for us, complete with roasted pig and hula dancers." During the social, he decided to explore a nearby mountain cave and discovered a World War II bayonet, which he treasures. Such times of recreation were the exception rather than the rule, though; the airmen, especially the pilots, spent most of their time working or sleeping. After Guam, Freeman returned to Columbus Air Force Base. He was there when he received his discharge, following four years of active duty.

Freeman came home to Madison. He worked for a while with Sears, pulling orders. He then attended Rockingham Community College on the GI Bill, earning an associate business degree. Initially, Zarn, a plastics company that also made canteens and other products for the military, employed him. Eventually, Zarn reorganized and moved away from the area. Consequently, Freeman went to work for Halstead Metal Products, where he actually assisted in the construction of the building. That completed, he went to Arkansas to learn to operate their equipment.

When Halstead was also sold and restructured, Freeman found employment with Bassett-Walker, supervising textile workers. Again, the company was bought and reformed. "I've had *good* jobs," opines Freeman, "but they always sell the business out from under me." His last position was with Frontier Spinning, where he served fourteen years before retiring.

Freeman married Brenda Simpson on December 16, 1972. They currently live in Mayodan with their daughter, Ashley.

Fred Gann

All told, I couldn't have gone in at a better time.

It was February 1954. Eighteen-year-old Fred Gann of Madison had just graduated high school. He decided to sign up for the Army rather than wait around and be drafted. He was sent to Fort Jackson, South Carolina, for a week of tests. From there, he went to Camp Gordon, Georgia, for eight weeks of basic training and then on to Camp Chaffee, Arkansas, for technical school. He was assigned to the motor pool.

"All told, I couldn't have gone in at a better time," figures Gann. "I was in Korea less than one year after the ceasefire was signed, and I left Fort Bragg to come home just as the war with Vietnam was heating up."

Gann was in Korea four months. "There was a big mountain, then another and another and another: it was *all* mountain," he recalls. Stationed near the thirty-eighth parallel—the Korean demilitarized zone— he worked as a carpenter, erecting structures around the compound, including headquarters for the officers. He also drove a water truck, collecting purified water from a pond or creek and delivering it to both the officers' and enlisted men's mess halls.

Gann, who at times interacted with indigenous personnel, recalls a Korean tailor who worked at the barracks, performing various sewing duties for the GIs. Koreans were not allowed to keep American currency, but this resourceful gentleman stashed some away in his sewing machine, as well as on his person. Before he left the camp, military police searched him and retrieved the money. "I thought they should have let him keep it," reasons Gann. "He earned it."

After Korea, Gann traveled to Camp Drake, a joint US Army/Air Force base just outside Tokyo, Japan. He was amazed to find the area largely rebuilt, with numerous tall buildings. His assignment was to make improvements around the compound. One of his favorite memories from that period has to do with professional baseball players whose careers had been interrupted by the draft. Charley Rayburn was one such athlete. Apparently, he had no official work assignment but spent his time traveling from place to place playing ball for the Army.

A visiting general, executing inspection on the troops, approached Rayburn and asked, "Soldier, what is your job?"

"I don't know; I give up," quipped Rayburn.

Needless to say, this response caused great embarrassment to the company commanders, who in turn presented Rayburn with a paintbrush and announced, "You are now in the Battery Improvement Section."

While in Japan, Gann enjoyed nine weeks of instruction in cooking and baking at beautiful Camp Eta Jima in Hiroshima Bay. This spacious, modern facility, which featured terraced gardens and a baseball field, had been a Japanese Naval Academy before being acquired by the United States. From that luxurious oasis, he returned to the Ninth Corps Artillery at Camp Drake, where he was promoted to corporal.

"When I came back to Fort Bragg for my last seven months of service, things were already heating up in Southeast Asia. We had been told to be ready to move out at any moment." Gann could not help but be apprehensive. He speculated at the time, "I just have a few days to go, but my time could be extended; I *could* be sent to a hot spot." Fortunately that did not happen, and he was discharged on February 1, 1957.

Gann returned to Rockingham County, and four months later, on July 2, 1957, he married Fay Nelson, also of Madison. He worked as a carpenter for a couple of months but eventually joined Madison Throwing Company, where he remained until his retirement thirty-eight years later. The Ganns have two sons, Jeffrey and Freddy. They also have one grandchild, currently a student at Radford University in Radford, Virginia.

Dan Greene

Kennedy was with our outfit in July of 1963, real close—elbow to elbow—and then he was assassinated in November.

"Our nation was in the most danger it has ever been in. We had a rocket loaded, ready to launch," assures Dan Greene of Troy. The Soviet Union—lagging behind the United States in the arms race—had conceived a plan to install intermediate-range missiles on the island of Cuba as a deterrent to a US attack against their homeland. President John F. Kennedy learned of the missile buildup on October 15, 1962. On October 22, he announced to the world his decision to impose a naval quarantine around Cuba. He warned that any nuclear missile launched from the island would be considered an attack on the United States by the Soviet Union and demanded that all offensive weapons be removed from Cuba.

Greene, assigned to the Honest John Rocket Program, was one of the first to learn of the pending crisis. He and his commanding officer had been in the field, dealing with a problem concerning the gun crew. "We came back into the battery area and found chaos," recalls Greene, in his soft Southern drawl. "The crew was already packing. Within a few hours, we had everything needed for survival loaded onto truck beds: motor pool, mess hall, kitchen." Greene was part of an advance party charged with securing a location for the rocket launcher, should firing become necessary. The men remained on high alert while living in the woods along the border of Florida for the next three weeks. "The crisis was averted when Soviet premier Nikita Khrushchev agreed to dismantle the missiles and return them to the Soviet Union. The United States, in turn, promised not to invade Cuba."

The Honest John was an unguided 762-millimeter artillery rocket. It was transported from the depot to the launching site by truck and trailer in three parts—warhead, motor, and fins. "I was one of six men who assembled the rocket and mounted it on the launcher," explains Greene. The Honest John, simplest of all US nuclear weapons to operate, had an active range of twenty-five miles.

Greene had been drafted on November 30, 1961. He went through basic training in Fort Jackson, South Carolina, and from there traveled to Fort Sill, Oklahoma, for artillery training. His last nineteen months of active duty were spent in Fort Benning, Georgia; it was there he became part of a composite outfit that included Honest John Rockets. During Greene's tenure, the crew fired at least one rocket per year—usually on the Fourth of July. It was always a major event, with appearances by President John F. Kennedy and a host of other dignitaries, both domestic and foreign. In 1962, the president was so impressed when the crew made a direct hit on a target seventeen miles away that he awarded each of them a Presidential Award. "Kennedy was with our outfit in July of 1963, real close—elbow-to-elbow—and then he was assassinated in November," reports Greene, still saddened by the loss.

The specialist fourth class had a number of secondary responsibilities. He instructed officer candidate students in the proper use of field artillery, he was parts man and dispatcher for the motor pool, and he was assistant mail clerk. Twice, he was recognized as soldier of the month; and nine times, he won the Driver Rodeo—an obstacle course maneuvered by vehicles pulling trailers. Greene's outfit routinely set up displays in neighboring towns, demonstrating the importance of various articles of military equipment.

He was separated from active duty in November 1963, but because of his Military Occupational Specialty, he was required to remain attached to the military for the next four years, during which time he *could* have been reactivated at any time. Meanwhile, he spent two weeks each summer at a

National Guard unit in Charleston, South Carolina, instructing soldiers destined for Vietnam in the use of 106-millimeter recoilless weapons, better known as bazookas. He taught them how to mount the weapons on quarter-ton jeeps, get the vehicles in place, zero in on targets, and fire the weapons. In October 1967, he received his final discharge from the military.

Before being drafted, Greene had moved to Greensboro to work with Sears Mail Order. He returned there briefly after coming home, but in 1979, he started his own business. He and his brother, along with their forty-five employees, did drywall, plaster, and acoustical ceilings for commercial buildings throughout North Carolina, South Carolina, and parts of Virginia. "When the economic downturn of the mid-eighties made it difficult to collect payment for our services," he says, "we closed the business, and I accepted an offer from the city of Greensboro to become building maintenance supervisor for twenty-three buildings." He oversaw a crew of six men for twenty years, retiring in November 2003.

Lane Rierson, Greene's first wife and mother of his children—Tammy, Dana, and Christina—passed away in 1989. In 2003, he married Evelyn Nichols and relocated to her hometown of Summerfield. He remains active in veterans' affairs.

Howard Gurley

We lost eighty pilots—killed in action. We
paid a terrible price for freedom!

From his first flight on December 20, 1943, until his last on May 7, 1945—one day before the war in Germany ended—Howard Gurley of Baltimore, Maryland, flew an astounding 141 combat missions, earning two Distinguished Flying Crosses and promotion to major in the process. Drafted into the Army in July 1941, he was assigned to the Ninth Infantry Division at Fort Bragg. Five months later, on December 7, the Japanese attacked Pearl Harbor. Gurley heard that the Army Air Corps was looking to expand its program by training additional pilots, bombardiers, and navigators. This appealed to him more than becoming a private in the Infantry, so he went to Pope Field and took the necessary tests to enter pilot training.

Ironically, although Gurley had orders transferring him from the Infantry to the Army Air Corps, he remained attached to the Ninth Infantry. "I could have been shipped out at any time; I was really relieved when I got word that I was being transferred to Vernon, Texas, to enter the pilot program." In March 1943, after he had spent nine months in intensive training, his wife, Marie Svec Gurley, whom he had married while stationed at Fort Bragg, pinned the coveted silver wings on his uniform.

Gurley was assigned to the 358th Fighter Group out of Richmond, Virginia. They flew P-47 Thunderbolts—large, single-engine fighter planes. In late 1943, they sailed to England in a military convoy, keeping careful watch for German submarines that had sunk a number of American ships in the Atlantic Ocean. Their initial mission was to escort heavy bombers from the Eighth Air Force. Later, Gurley was transferred to the Ninth Air Force, where he flew low-level missions—attacking trains, tanks, and enemy forces in support of General Patton's war against the Germans.

Gurley's first combat mission was to fly cover for a flight of B-17 bombers. His orders were to fly over the North Sea and rendezvous with the bombers over Holland, at an altitude of approximately eighteen thousand feet. There were forty-eight planes in the cover group—three squadrons of sixteen. Fighter planes were limited to three hundred gallons of gasoline, and they burned ninety gallons per hour. Therefore, they carried full external tanks in case additional fuel was needed. The external tanks, however, had no fuel gauges. Pilots had to remember when they switched to external tanks and keep track of their time.

Gurley's squadron met the bombers—hundreds of B-17s—over Holland. They had just made their formation above them when Gurley's engine quit. "The silence was deafening," he says. Soon, he was left alone in the enemy sky over Holland. "I lost several thousand feet of altitude and held a dead stick in my hand. I remember thinking, 'All that time and training, and I'm going to crash in Holland on my very first mission.'" Just in time, however, he realized that he had forgotten to switch tanks. The external tank he was using had run dry, and an air lock had formed in the carburetor. "The engine eventually restarted, but all I could think of at the time was 'I have aborted my very first mission, with a perfectly-flying plane and no flak damage. *They will think I lost my nerve.*'"

On January 14, 1945, Gurley was leading a squadron of twelve planes on a bombing mission to Winden, Germany, near the Rhine River, their target a group of warehouses used as a supply dump. Each plane carried five-hundred-pound bombs beneath both wings. Eight pilots prepared to drop their deadly loads, while four positioned themselves to provide top cover.

Suddenly Gurley's plane was hit by fire from a German Messerschmitt 109. Smoke filled the cockpit. "For a split second, I did not realize what had happened. My first instinct was to kick the left rudder and pop the stick. Actually, my right wing tip had been blown off. There was damage to my left wing, engine cowling, and radio compartment. Miraculously, I still had control of the plane.

"When the smoke cleared, I could see a plane below me. It was Fred Bishop, one of our cover men. He had warned us to 'break,' but we had not heard him. Thomson, our number four man, was also hit. He tried unsuccessfully to crash land; his body was later recovered from the charred remains of his plane. Both Bishop and I made it back to our base in Toul, France."

On June 7, 1944—D-day plus one, Gurley's group was flying cover for a flight of gliders. Each glider was carrying approximately twenty men to the battlefront on Normandy beach. "We were flying at somewhere around five thousand feet, while the gliders were being towed by C-47s at a height of one thousand feet. There was not enough room for all of them to touch down. After being cut loose from their towlines, they began to float downward toward the earth. I watched, horrified, as gliders crashed into each other while trying to land." According to Gurley, "Actual footage of the tragedy is shown in the movie *Saving Private Ryan*."

One of Gurley's most frightening experiences occurred when he and the flight of four he was leading mistakenly landed in the wrong country. "We thought we were over England, but instead we were over France. While we were still above Normandy, we saw what we believed to be the correct landing field beneath us. We began to descend, but when we buzzed the field to drop our wheels and flaps, we started receiving ground fire. 'Where the hell are we?' I wondered out loud. All we had to guide us was a high altitude map spread across our knees."

Low on fuel, the airmen were forced to work their way back across the English Channel to England. They began transmitting "Mayday, Mayday," the international distress call. "One of our pilots, Norman Averett, bailed out," says Gurley. "He opened his canopy, stood up, and dove for the wing; instead, he hit the tail of the airplane. He managed, despite a broken back, to get a dinghy underneath him and hold on until British Air Sea Rescue came and got him. Another pilot, Art Charbonneau, also bailed out and was picked up by a British ship. The fourth pilot, Jim Gray, and I made our way back through the Isle of Wight to our base in southern England, where Gray's plane had to be towed off the runway."

When the war in Europe ended, on May 8, 1945, the 358th was supposed to be transferred to the Pacific, but while Gurley was on leave in Baltimore, that war ended also. The outfit was sent to La Junta, Colorado, for additional training, and from there to Denver for assignment. While in Denver, Gurley was released from active duty, having accumulated the required number of points.

He returned to his job with Western Electric and was eventually transferred to Greensboro. He and Marie (now deceased) have three sons, three daughters, and nine grandchildren. Gurley reflects on his military career: "We lost eighty pilots—killed in action; we paid a terrible price for freedom!"

Major Howard L. Gurley died April 15, 2009, shortly after talking with the author.

Jake Hopper

When I went in, they were taking everything. They took one guy who was completely blind in one eye.

Eleven-year-old Jake Hopper had no way of knowing that falling out the door and puncturing his left eye on a stake would one day necessitate his being placed on limited military service, dictating that due to physical disability, he would not enter combat unless doing so became unavoidable. "When I went in, they were taking everything," he explains. "They took one guy who was completely blind in one eye." The future private first class would spend his entire tenure—eleven and a half months—at Camp McCain in Granada, Mississippi, attached to the Fourth Service Command, Military Police (MP).

"I was one of those guys who wore white leggings and gloves and stood at the gate," offers Hopper. "I monitored traffic and checked credentials of individuals going on and off base." The next gate was two miles away, and there were no lights. He admits that sometimes the loneliness, coupled with the darkness, left him feeling a little vulnerable. He encountered few problems, however, except for drunken GIs returning from Memphis after a long weekend: "Some would be loud and disorderly; others passed out on the floor of the Trailways bus, but their buddies usually offered to take care of them. I never had to actually call the paddy wagon; I just had to use a little common sense.

"Still, a frightening situation did arise on one occasion. I received a tip that a soldier had gone AWOL and was at the home of a local farmer asking for civilian clothes. As required, I reported this information to the provost marshal, who, along with a captain, hurried to the farm." The fugitive ran, prompting an order to "stop him!" A shot rang out, followed closely by the appearance of a speeding ambulance. "I knew the GI had been hit. Fortunately, the wound was not fatal, but a threat was made against *me*, due to my involvement in the incident. The number of guards at the gate was doubled until the danger passed."

Hopper was drafted in October 1942 and discharged in November 1943, after developing a troublesome ulcer. He had not been home since his induction and was anxious to see his family. He caught a train to Roanoke, Virginia, and thumbed a ride on an empty gas tanker from there to Madison. He had cultivated a moustache, but fearing his mother would disapprove, he decided to have it shaved off before surprising his parents, who were unaware of his release. He stopped by the local barbershop, and "Who do you think was in the chair?" he asks. "My father!" Together, father and son returned to their home, where for the next year, Hopper observed prescribed dietary regulations and medication to restore his health.

He married Barbara Jefferies, with whom he has one son, Eugene—a poliomyelitis survivor who spent nine months in a hospital, gaining control of the disease. Hopper put his law enforcement training to use with the Reidsville Police Department for one year before being hired by the Department of Agriculture to work with soil and conservation. Prior to being transferred to Rockingham County, he worked for extended periods in Ahoskie, Roxboro, and Greensboro. He retired in 1984, following thirty years of service. Regrettably, he lost his wife after forty-two years of marriage.

On February 10, 1995, Hopper married Virginia Tate, a widow with three children. They currently make their home in Madison, where they remain active in community affairs and enjoy their children, grandchildren, and great-grandchildren.

Rudolph Joyce

Amid smoke and whirling debris, I recognized body parts—
arms and legs—floating on the water. And jeeps, their brakes
no longer working, plowed helplessly over falling soldiers.

O n D-day, Mayodan's Rudolph Joyce was responsible for dropping the ramp on the landing craft tank, permitting infantrymen and vehicles to enter the waters off Omaha Beach. The crew had sailed from Portsmouth the day before, June 5, 1944, but threatening weather and choppy waters in the English Channel had delayed the offensive. They traveled in a convoy, with minesweepers leading the way and balloons hovering overhead to discourage attack from enemy planes. German occupying forces, anticipating action by the Americans, had constructed four lines of obstacles in the water, each equipped with deadly wires and mines. Additionally, Allied planes had created huge craters beneath the surface when they bombed and strafed in an effort to eliminate the obstructions before landing occurred. As a result, the two-hundred-yard span the GIs were forced to maneuver to make shore was riddled with peril. Joyce could hear the din of battle before they approached the drop-off point.

He watched comrades, weighted down with heavy backpacks, sink into the neck-deep waters as they struggled to maintain their footing while dodging the traps that exploded all around them. Men and vehicles disappeared into deep chasms: some resurfaced; others were forever lost to the sea. Joyce describes the scene: "Amid smoke and whirling debris,

I could recognize body parts—arms and legs—floating on the water. And jeeps, their brakes no longer working, plowed helplessly over falling soldiers."

He had gotten to know many of the soldiers participating in the assault, and one said to him, "I don't think I will be going back home. I wonder if it wouldn't be good if you would take my money and send it to my family." Joyce hesitated, not wanting to convey the notion that he too considered the young man's death imminent.

"Oh Jimmy, don't worry about it," he reassured. "You'll be all right." But Jimmy was not all right; he was one of the first to die. Joyce confesses, "I will always wonder whether or not I made the right decision."

Those who made it to the beach were met with overwhelming resistance and took heavy casualties. They were hit with small arms, mortars, and artillery. German artillerymen hiding in concrete pillboxes operated machine guns from relative safety. So determined were the Germans to stop the invasion at the beaches that no area was left unprotected. Only through sheer numbers of troops were the Americans able to advance. Thousands lost their lives.

As Joyce looked out over the slaughter, bullets bounced off the two-inch shield that surrounded his cubicle. "The noise was deafening. If I had not had earphones, I could not have heard the skipper's orders," he reasons. When all the troops and equipment were unloaded, he raised the ramp, and the craft returned to the merchant ship in the bay to pick up additional men and supplies.

"Things were quieter that first night," he recalls. "They were moving inland. The last troops did not have the same problems on the beach, but they were fighting further in." In a couple of days, despite tremendous hardship, the area was secured and the objectives achieved. The sailors continued to bring in medical supplies, food, and ammunition. Soldiers transferred the goods to Army trucks and hauled them to supply dumps.

After the fighting ended, the skipper addressed his men: "Now I can't tell you to do this, but if *I* were *you*, I would go into town a few at a time.

If you get caught, you will be considered AWOL, but I will be the officer in charge, so I'll take care of you." The skipper also recommended that they "empty their gas masks and fill them with candy and cigarettes." The men, of course, did as suggested, entering town in groups of six.

"The villagers welcomed us warmly," says Joyce. "Stores were open, and I traded cigarettes and candy for trinkets. Cigarettes were especially valuable.

"When all of our duties were completed, we held a memorial service to honor those who lost their lives in the attack and its aftermath. We were praised by our high command and assured the rest of our Navy duty would be stateside." On the strength of that promise, Joyce used his six-week leave to marry his longtime sweetheart, Betty Wilson, also of Mayodan. "Six months later, I began tours in the Marshall Islands, Guam, Tinnean, and Saipan. After that, I was a little skeptical of promises made on the basis of assumptions. But the fighting was largely over when I arrived in the Pacific.

"I mainly transported supplies—a large number of which consisted of wooden cases labeled 'Carrot Juice.' One day, one of the cases fell through the net while being transferred from cargo ship to transport vessel. That was when we discovered we had been carrying *whiskey*. The skipper told us, 'Every time we bring carrot juice, put one case in the forward hold, and we will have it.' After the fighting was over, we traded whiskey for steaks for months. We probably ate better than anyone in the Navy."

Joyce concedes that his most frightening moments came not from the heat of battle, but from riding out a typhoon in Okinawa. He tells of water gushing over the sides of the craft, while wind-blasted sailors strained to carry out their duties—holding onto the rails of the ship with one hand. "The flat-bottomed vessel was not designed to be seagoing: gales lifted it high into the air, and then—*BAM*—the steel deck slammed into the churning waters with such force that it quivered and shook.

"The ships were close together, and all had their anchors out to help resist wind pressure. Another ship beat against us until it finally knocked a hole in our side. We stuffed mattresses and timbers into the breach. We donned life jackets, realizing we may be forced to abandon ship. I prayed that would not happen, knowing lives could be lost to the huge, spinning propellers." Mercifully, the storm abated, and the violent waters grew calm.

Joyce was in Sasebo, Japan, when he acquired the necessary points to separate from the Navy. He returned to Mayodan, where he resumed work in the Washington Mills office. The bosun's mate second class had undergone life-altering experiences since receiving his draft notice two years earlier: he had traveled to Bainbridge, Maryland, for boot camp; transferred to Solomon Island for small boat and landing craft instruction; and then moved on to Little Creek, Virginia, for assignment to an LCT training ship before being deployed to the European Theatre, where he came face-to-face with death and dying.

Back home, Joyce soon grew restless in the mill office and asked to be transferred to the machine department. Still dissatisfied, he decided to take advantage of the GI Bill and entered the Kansas City School of Horology, Kansas City, Missouri, to study watch repair. After graduating and working an apprenticeship with brother-in-law Roy Humphrey, a Reidsville jeweler, he opened a jewelry store in nearby Madison. A few years later, he purchased property in a local shopping center and built Rudolph's Jewelry, which he operated until his retirement.

Rudolph and Betty Joyce have one daughter, Jan Streeter, and two grandsons, Mason and Maxton. Maxton recently returned from a tour of duty in Afghanistan.

Caleb King

I was so scared; I thought I was shaking the whole island.

He was not yet twenty-one, too young to enlist in the US military; at least, that is what Caleb King of Madison was told when he attempted to do just that. Imagine his surprise when he received his draft notice before celebrating his next birthday. He took his physical examination in June 1942 and was called to active duty the following November.

King was sent to Camp Wheeler, Georgia, for thirteen weeks of basic training. From there he went to Camp Stoneman, California, where he remained for four or five days before taking a boat down the San Joaquin River to the docks in San Francisco. On April 4, 1943, he boarded a ship to New Caledonia for assignment to the 169th Infantry, 43rd Division. After a stop at Guadalcanal, he traveled to Munda, in the Northern Solomons, to join A Company, First Battalion. "Only eighteen men remained in the company, which held around 150 at maximum strength. I was one of thirty-nine replacements," he says.

He was carried directly to the front line. On his first day of battle, as the company moved up a hill in single file, the man directly behind him was suddenly shot and killed. "Before I had time to recover from that shock, the man directly in front of me was killed. I was so scared; I thought I was shaking the whole island. From that time forward, our routine was pretty much the same. We would advance as far as possible during daylight hours, pushing the Japanese back as we went; dig a foxhole just before dark; crawl into it; and stay there until the sun came up. We had an understanding: anything seen moving at night was a target. If anyone got out of his foxhole, *he* became the enemy.

"Unless we were cut off from supplies—which happened a lot—we requisitioned enough food at one time to last us three days. Sometimes we lived on coconuts and Japanese rice, sometimes on nothing at all." Day after day, King, a machine gunner—accompanied by his assistant gunner and two ammunitions carriers—inched forward, cradling twenty-eight-pound guns and backpacking picks and shovels for "digging in" when night fell. With little rest and often hungry, they did their best to support each other physically and emotionally.

Foxholes had to be large enough to house two to three occupants, and King, over six feet tall, had to make his accommodate his length. "We took turns sleeping," he explains, "one of us always watching for the enemy. Sometimes a man panicked and had to be held in the pit, although being dug in was no guarantee against being hit. One time there were three of us in a hole and two were killed."

Sometimes Japanese soldiers jumped into American foxholes wielding machetes. When the GIs began to fight back, using their own knives, the Japanese jumped out of the holes, leaving the confused Americans slashing at each other. This prompted a ruling against having more than one blade in a foxhole.

"About dusk one evening, four of us were sleeping on the ground when Japanese soldiers opened fire, killing all except me. Two of them died instantly, but the other suffered late into the night. I did everything I could to help him," reflects King. "The medic had bandaged his arm but overlooked a more serious injury to his side. I will never forget watching that soldier breathe through a hole in his side. His breaths just came shorter and shorter. I waited for first light, then crawled over the stiffening bodies and pushed on."

On another occasion, King and members of his company were sleeping on the ground in a heavily wooded area. They awakened to the sound of Japanese voices closing in on them. King remembers, "We began to lob hand grenades: one, two, three—we threw seven in all. Then we started shooting. My weapon jammed: the ammunition was supposed to lie flat, but instead curled into rolls, causing the gun to misfire. We couldn't see a thing. We just fired in the direction of the voices. The chatter eventually stopped, and we could tell from the amount of blood that they had been hit hard. But Japanese soldiers dragged their dead off to prevent us from knowing how many were killed, so we never got a body count.

"When one of our own was killed, we dug a shallow grave and laid the body in it, placing one of his dog tags around his neck and the other on a stick to mark the grave. After the battle ended, someone in the company went with a gravedigger to show him where the body rested. The fallen soldier would then be buried in a cemetery. Later, if requested, the body could be returned to the soldier's family."

Those on the front line were constantly aware of impending death. Whenever possible, they held church services. King kept a New Testament his father had given him in the lining of his helmet and prayed often for safety. "Once," he confides, "God spoke to me. I was out of the hole, and they [the Japanese] started throwing artillery. I jumped in a hole with two more boys. I remember that one of them had a pot of instant coffee; he told me not to turn it over. While I was in the hole, a shell hit below it and injured one of the guys. The Good Lord told me to 'get out of there,' and I did. I have never heard anything plainer in my whole life. The next shell that came over killed that boy. The shells were so thick it felt like you could stick your helmet up and catch them. Amazingly, although the hole was blown completely apart, that pot of coffee was still intact.

"I took part in one landing—Luzon—in June of 1945. We entered at Lingayen Gulf, where the ramp of our landing craft failed to drop. We scrambled over the sides into the water and waded onto the beach. The Filipinos greeted us, waving victory signs. Then the Japanese opened fire, hitting four of the ten in our group. I helped one of the wounded to safety. We worked our way down to Manila and stayed at Clark Field twenty-six days." Asked to describe the encounters that followed, he states simply, "We wiped them out."

King was involved in clearing tunnels where Japanese soldiers remained hidden. "I was nervous as a rat when I got in one of those tunnels," he admits. "Some of the guys enjoyed searching them for souvenirs, but I was no souvenir hunter; I wanted to *live*. However, I did spot a coveted Japanese flag. When I went to pick it up, I saw a yellow wire attached. It was booby-trapped; I just backed away and left it there."

He shares the experience of a friend who was exploring a tunnel when, unexpectedly, everything went black. "My buddy yelled, 'Get out of the light!' In response, a Japanese soldier committed suicide, falling dead right in front of him. He had been standing in the passageway, blocking the light."

King was in the Philippines when he heard that the Japanese had surrendered. He had been overseas thirty months and twenty-six days. For the first six months of 1945, he had slept on a cot only twenty nights. "Otherwise, I sacked out in foxholes or on the ground," he explains. Except for thirty-day R&R leaves in New Zealand, he had spent his entire deployment on the front line. He achieved the rank of staff sergeant. The enemy never hit King, an astounding statistic considering seven of every ten men killed during World War II were Infantry. He did, however, suffer recurring bouts of malaria.

King was awarded numerous medals, including three Battle Participant Stars for the Northern Solomons, New Guinea, and the Philippines; the prestigious Combat Infantryman Badge, which earned him an additional ten dollars each month; and a Bronze Service Arrowhead for the assault landing in Luzon. He was recognized as being among the first forces to go into Japan and establish occupancy of Honshu.

After his discharge on November 12, 1945, King came home, where for many months he relived the terrors of war through nightmares. He worked a short while with locally owned Gem Dandy, Inc., and then rebuilt automobile starters for a Winston-Salem-based company. Eventually, he joined Sears Roebuck in Greensboro, where he remained until his retirement forty years later. On March 1, 1947, King married Nancy Snead, also of Madison. The union produced two children: son

David Snead King and daughter Jane King Ward, who currently teaches school in Orange Park, Florida.

Caleb King died on May 4, 2008, a couple of weeks after he shared his stories with the author. Nancy preceded him in death (August 9, 1985), as did David (May 4, 2004).

James Abraham King Jr.

I consider myself a scrounge officer.

"RETIRED & BROKE DRIVE," "SLOW, GRANDPARENTS AT PLAY," "BORDER COLLIE XING"—I find myself smiling at the phrases printed on the signboards that greet me as I maneuver my PT Cruiser up the long, winding, gravel road that leads to the expansive Stoneville residence of James Abraham King Jr. Soon, the Greensboro native and I are seated next to each other in his comfortable family room, chatting easily about his experiences in the United States Air Force.

"I consider myself a scrounge officer," he explains. That thought inspires a barrage of related memories that leapfrog each other as they tumble nimbly from his lips. I grab hold of what seems to be an important detail, inserted almost as an afterthought: "My position was listed as engineer." Truth be told, the resourceful lieutenant was far better known for his ability to cut through red tape and get the job done—no questions asked.

King graduated Admiral Farragut Naval Academy in Saint Petersburg, Florida, before attending North Carolina State University from 1951 until 1955. There, during the depths of the Korean War, he participated in Air Force Reserve Officers' Training Corps. Because of his grade point average (3.0), he was deferred from the draft so that he could complete his education. He would later enter the Air Force as a commissioned officer.

After college, King worked for a company in Pennsylvania, but knowing he would soon receive military orders, he maintained his Greensboro address. For over five years, he had dated Joan Hester, a Woman's College student. When his summons finally arrived, his father opened it—as prearranged—and telephoned his son with the news that he was going to Britain. "I decided it would be good to marry before deploying, but one major hurdle remained: I had not yet proposed. My father offered to play Cupid and pop the question for me. He must have been persuasive. The next telephone call I received was from Joan, telling me how wonderful it was that we were getting married."

The nuptials took place in Greensboro on March 31, 1956—the twenty-fifth wedding anniversary of the groom's parents. Joan graduated in late July and followed her husband overseas in August. King says, "We had a two year honeymoon in Cambridge, England, paid for by US taxpayers." Since there was no base housing, the couple lived on the British economy, renting an upstairs flat in the home of an older couple and shopping in local stores for food and goods.

King, who received no basic training due to the aforementioned ROTC involvement, joined the ranks of the Royal Air Force Station in Alconbury, England, in April 1956. Their objective was to bring a World War II bomber base up to jet standards. His first assignment was to serve as air installation officer in the motor maintenance office; his second was to make English power work with an AM generator. He was also called on to repair plumbing and anything else that went awry.

King was soon promoted to first lieutenant, that position having been recently vacated. He was delighted to learn that a former classmate—a construction engineer—would become his second lieutenant. The two formed an effective team, King performing mechanical and electrical chores, while his friend addressed civil engineering tasks.

The Korean War ended in 1953; the Vietnam War did not begin until 1959. King, therefore, never battled an enemy on foreign soil. A couple of noteworthy events did take place on the national scene during his tenure, however, that brought the base to full alert: in 1956, President

Gamal A. Nasser of Egypt wrenched control of the Suez Canal from the British in a bloodless coup, and in 1957, the Soviet Union launched the world's first artificial satellite, Sputnik 1, into space. Otherwise, peace reigned throughout his military career, leaving him free to forage about—perfecting the delicate art of scrounging.

King remembers one occasion when his immediate supervisor approached him with a dilemma. "The mess hall was in dire need of new furnishings, and he wondered if I could be of assistance in the matter. And by the way, he just happened to know of a base group that was scheduled to shut down." The crafty lieutenant began immediately to devise a scheme. He selected a crew of willing associates and finagled four Suburbans and seven flatbed tractor-trailer trucks. With these, he set out for the Royal Air Force Station at Holme-on-Spalding-Moor.

The stealthy crew walked boldly onto the air base around five o'clock in the afternoon, deliberately neglecting to check in. They toured the area, shopped the PX, ate dinner in the chow hall, and attended a base movie. They waited until all personnel assigned to that base had left for the night and then sprang into action. *Everything* was confiscated: grills, ranges, dishwashers, serving lines, trays. They stripped the building, burning pipes off at the floor. At four o'clock in the morning, they loaded the tractor- trailers and took off for Alconbury.

"You just *took* it?" I ask, searching my mind for a more tenable explanation.

"Now you're catching on," he shoots back with a mischievous nod.

From time to time, other strange happenings occurred around the Alconbury station, such as the heretofore-unattainable flagpole that suddenly appeared out of nowhere, casting its tall shadow across the landscape.

Eventually, King was assigned to the Fourth Tactical Depot Squadron, a top-secret project involving special weaponry. A cyclone fence, guard towers, and dogs protected the area. No one went in or out without a special identification card. Apparently, this restrictive environment only served to enhance King's ability to avoid going through normal channels to produce desired results. "Scrounging was much easier there," he insists. "Once I got what I needed through the gate, no one ever saw it again, nor could they come in and look for it."

King discovered a forty-by-one-hundred-foot Butler Building "just occupying space in the storage area—in case war broke out in Europe." With a little creative paperwork, he managed to lay claim to it. He uncrated the building and "borrowed" enough ready-mix concrete to pour footings and flooring, plus a spray booth of paint intended for an eighteen-wheel truck. Presently, an officers' club emerged. "I just put it into *vertical* storage," jests King, who also turned a Quonset hut into a ready room, where the staff could assemble to receive orders and instructions. It was furnished with tables, desks, chairs, and snack bar.

Resident golfers encouraged King to construct a golf course within the compound. He agreed on *one* condition: enlisted men must be allowed to play the course. That settled, he proceeded to lay out the links between and around existing weapons bunkers. Twenty baggage trailers were converted into golf carts.

The Kings enjoyed their stay in England and remember their associates, friends, and experiences with smiles and affection. They left December 17, 1957, when he received a reduction-in-force discharge. They returned to Greensboro, where he joined his father at J. A. King Company, distributors of industrial scale and weight equipment, founded by the senior King in 1939. King Jr. remained with the partnership forty-one years before retiring on December 31, 1998. One of his two sons currently operates the business. The couple also has three daughters and twelve grandchildren.

Meanwhile, I have it on good authority that, when the occasion presents itself, King can still scrounge with the best of them.

William Knight

I lay a lot of nights and prayed that things would work out.

"I'm sure that any boy scout can outmarch me," admits William Knight, who, after being drafted into the Army Air Force on September 4, 1942, received only one week of basic training at Fort Bragg. "I was there three weeks," explains the Madison native, "but two were spent doing paperwork." That ordeal completed, he embarked on a whirlwind tour of Army bases and training centers. His first stop was Keesler Field in Biloxi, Mississippi, where upon completion of aptitude tests, he was given a choice of training to be radio operator, engineer, or armament specialist. He opted for armament school at Buckley Field in Denver, Colorado. "I thought that would be a lot cooler," he said. "I just wanted to get away from the heat."

After Denver, Knight was sent to Las Vegas for five weeks of gunnery school, the last of which was spent shooting at low targets from an airplane. While there, he was promoted to staff sergeant. From that vacation paradise, he proceeded to Salt Lake City, Utah, to await assignment. Temporary housing was made available at the luxurious fairgrounds: "The building contained six rows of one hundred cots each, and I had a time figuring out which one was mine," recalls Knight.

At Davis Air Force Base in Tucson, Arizona, Knight was assigned to a crew, and they began learning to fly heavy bombers (B-24s) together. Training was completed in Pocatello, Idaho, after which they were given a nine-day "delay in route" before reporting to Topeka, Kansas, to board an airplane for overseas.

"Today," he reasons, "that trip could be made in one hop, but at that time, we could only go so far before having to touch down. Our destination was New Guinea, but we made stops in San Francisco, Hawaii, Australia, Christmas Island, Aquila Island, Fiji Island, and New Caledonia. It took us *months* to get to the Air Force base on Port Moresby, one of the few places in New Guinea not already controlled by Japanese forces." From that location, tail-gunner Knight and his crew would fly bombing and reconnaissance missions into New Guinea and New Britain.

On their first scouting assignment, the bombardier sank two enemy merchant ships. When this became known, they were made lead plane in the squadron. "When we had completed six months, we were supposed to come home, but there were no replacements, so we had to stay," reports the Distinguished Flying Cross recipient. He flew fifty-five missions, each carefully recorded in a personal diary. The following excerpts are taken from his own notes, written shortly after completion of each operation:

> My first mission of August 20, 1943: we were flying the "Scorpion," loaded with six thousand lbs. of bombs, which we dropped on Boram Airfield, starting large fires. As we started over the target, ack-ack was popping everywhere, zero all around. B-24 behind our ship on fire—went down in flames. Parachutes opened up. Baker got a zero. The P-38 fighter plane shot down; a twin-engine plane at 5:00. The pilot bailed out. Seven and three-tenth hours later, we landed safely on our airfield.

> It was Oct. 12, 1943, that we started out to make a strike on Rabaul. My crew was flying "Patches" loaded with six thousand lbs. of bombs to drop on the harbor. There were ninety-eight B-25s and one hundred P-38s, with eighty-six Liberator bombers. One hundred and twenty-

six enemy planes lost, five warships sunk with 117 other vessels. All planes returned to base but five. After eight hours of hard flying, we landed with one hundred and fifty gallons of gas left.

On Dec. 1, 1943, we made our twentieth mission, in which we flew "Naughty Blue Eyes" loaded with forty one-hundred-lb. bombs. Our target was Wewak supply dump. The target was really set on fire. There were plenty of ack-ack and zero. My waist gunner and I got our first zeros. One B-24 went down over target. One plane in our squadron got two engines out, and we covered them until they went down in the water. Six men got out of the crash. We dropped supplies to them and left. The mission was nine hours long, and one that I will never forget.

Our twenty-first mission on Dec. 2, 1943: we flew "Naughty Blue Eyes" on a search for the boys in the raft. We found them and covered them until they were picked up at 5:30 p.m. Then we returned to our home base after being in the air for eight hours with nothing to eat or drink all day, but that was better than being on the life raft.

On Dec. 28, 1943, I made my thirtieth mission. Our target was ack-ack positions at Alexishafen. We were flying ship #135 loaded with six thousand lb. bombs, which we dropped at seventy-five-foot intervals, starting big fires that carried flames three thousand feet into the air. Just as we dropped our bombs, a burst of ack-ack sounded out under the tail of our plane. At the same time my right heel felt as if it had been hit by a rock about the size of my head. I didn't know whether I had been hurt or not, but luckily it just cut the leather on the heel of my shoe and caught in an empty cartridge case, causing it to stop without being able to go through a thin piece of metal right under my leg. Our height was fifteen thousand feet over target. Mission was five hours and fifteen minutes, and one I won't forget.

On March 8, 1944, we went on our forty-third mission. Our target was Dagua strip at Wewak. We were flying ship #131 loaded with eight thousand pounders. The target was covered over with clouds, and we had no fighter with us at the time. Zero started coming from everywhere at one time, there being twenty-five of them and twelve of us. Every gun on the plane was blasting at once. There were planes at every number on the clock. My crew altogether fired three thousand rounds of ammo getting three different planes and three propellers. The fight lasted for half an hour. We lost one plane of men in my group. We had to drop our bombs on the strips at Hansa Bay with a direct hit. There was ack-ack at both places. Several of the planes got holes in them. The mission was five hours and forty minutes.

On May 3, 1944, we made our forty-ninth mission. Our target was the strip of Boram. We were flying ship "Ready, Willing, and Able," loaded with eight thousand pounders. All bombs hit target. No ack-ack or enemy planes. Mission four hours and forty-five minutes long. Total 322:30 hours.

This was the last mission recorded in Knight's diary. He returned to the states and resumed his pre-overseas base hopping. Over the next year, he spent time in Nashville, Tennessee; Miami Beach, Florida; Denver,

Colorado; and Wichita Falls and Amarillo, Texas. Knight was discharged on November 1, 1945.

He returned to Madison and married Saula Rakestraw, whom he had met on a blind date during a thirty-day leave. He worked with his brother in a motel, farmed, and ran various convenience stores around the area before establishing William's Curb Market on Highway 220 in Madison. One of his five sons currently manages the business. The couple also has three daughters.

Reflecting on his wartime experience, Knight muses, "It changes you. I wouldn't take anything for it, but I wouldn't want to do it again. It seems like a dream." He pauses briefly and adds, "I lay a lot of nights and prayed that things would work out."

Olga "Dusty" Lathrop

I went in there and delivered a baby boy on Independence Day.

If war had not erupted, Dusty Lathrop's life might have taken a decidedly different turn. A singer, the New Jersey native planned to attend Juilliard and pursue a career in music. Desiring to gain poise and posture to enhance her opportunities, she accepted the offer made to her and two classmates to be trained and employed as showroom models. She was unprepared, however, for the vitriol directed toward her from friends of the terminated model she was hired to replace. "No thank you," she announced dramatically; "I don't have to put up with this." And she walked away, leaving the unmodeled clothes and her glamorous new career in her wake.

Music came naturally for Lathrop—then still known by her maiden name, Dusty Lewandowski— who played flute in the high school band. "My father [John Lewandowski] played first violin in the Metropolitan Opera House in New York City," she shares proudly. In fact, her parents spoke familiarly of Paderewski, piano virtuoso and frequent guest in their home *before* their immigration to America from Poland. Everything changed, however, on December 7, 1941, when the Japanese bombed Pearl Harbor. Always patriotic, as evidenced by her activities as air-raid warden while in high school, Lathrop wanted to serve her country further by joining the Navy, but—at nineteen—she did not meet the age requirement of twenty-one years.

Girlfriends persuaded Lathrop to accompany them to the Army recruiter's office. She agreed to complete their tests but insisted she was not interested in enlisting. An astute recruiter suggested she consider the Army Air Corps, their age requirement being twenty. This appealed to her, and after her next birthday, she went to Grand Central Station to enlist in the Women's Auxiliary Air Corps (WAAC). Soon thereafter, she boarded a train for Camp Oglethorpe, Georgia, to undergo basic training and instruction in nursing. Afterward, she traveled to Truax Field in Madison, Wisconsin, where she was assigned to the maternity ward of the base hospital.

One day, while returning to the hospital from the camp swimming pool, Lathrop missed her bus. As she stood helplessly, uniform on arm, shaking her fist at the disappearing bus, two impish GIs called out, "Come on, Dusty, we'll take you over to the hospital." She climbed into their jeep, grateful for the help.

"They took me on a wild ride, bouncing over fields and gullies; they wanted me to scream, but I wouldn't do it," she declares triumphantly. Finally, they arrived at their destination. "I was relaxing and drinking a glass of water when, all of a sudden, a sergeant rushed in shouting that his wife was having a baby."

Lathrop ran to the delivery room to tell the doctor, who, ironically, was in the midst of delivering his own wife's baby. "Just go get a tape and scissors, and go on in there until the relief doctor comes," he ordered.

"Well, I went in there," remembers Lathrop, "and delivered a baby boy on Independence Day. The relief doctor came in just as I was finishing up." The next day, the baby's maternal grandparents showed up with cake, strawberries, and whipped cream, wanting to meet the "little WAAC" who had delivered their grandson. Apparently, the doctor felt remorse at leaving Lathrop to perform a delivery alone because he told her she deserved to be transferred to the orthopedic ward. "That made me happy," she beams. "I just loved working with all those wounded and amputees."

She talks of trying to make friends with a noncommunicative amputee: "It was Christmas time, and I finally convinced him to let me write to his wife. Later, I got him into a wheelchair and pushed him to the theater to see Dennis Morgan. Dennis was finishing a song when a Red Cross woman came up and told him it was time for their party, so he went off without talking to us. I was pretty disgusted. I always worshipped Dennis Morgan, but if I saw him now, I would say, 'Dennis, you're a stinker.'"

On another occasion, while walking through the surgical ward, Lathrop stopped to watch a doctor pour sulfur on an open gunshot wound. "Doesn't that make you sick?" the doctor asked.

"No," she proclaimed, surprised at the question.

"Good," responded the doctor, "then you can stay here and help me."

After that, Lathrop assisted the doctors in addition to administering exercises and caring for her patients. An incident occurred, however, that made her consider—albeit momentarily—going AWOL. She had made friends with some young men who were in military flight school. They had been in training for only a short time when they were involved in an airplane crash. All aboard were killed.

"I was so upset. They were just nice young boys, and I could remember dancing with all of them. I wrote my cousin, a bombardier in North Africa, and told him I didn't think I wanted to be in the WAAC any longer. He telephoned and calmed me down. He reminded me that those things happen in war; we just have to keep going."

Lathrop learned the war had ended while being driven home after her hospital shift. "Where is everyone?" she asked.

"Haven't you heard? The war is over!" answered her driver.

"Well, no one told us at the hospital," she protested.

Lathrop's attention was suddenly diverted by a noisy band of revelers marching toward her hoisting a clothesline—complete with poles. "Oh my gosh!" she exclaimed. "*There go my undies.* I just hung them out this morning, and they are definitely *not* government issue." Her driver laughed so hard he almost ran over the curb. Sadly, her unmentionables were never returned. "Not even my silk stockings," she snaps.

After the war, Lathrop was transferred to Camp McCoy, a prisoner of war camp in Wisconsin. She requested and was granted assignment to the lab. "When I started to go up the stairs," she says, "two Japanese soldiers came running down. Well, I just stood there aghast."

"Missy, okay," they reassured, gesturing furiously. Shaken, Lathrop hurried into the lab, where workers noting her dismay questioned her about what had happened.

"Two Japanese without guards are running down the stairs!" she gasped, fully expecting a red alert to be sounded.

"So what?" they asked, nonplussed.

Obviously, the WAAC had landed in a situation that would require a mind-set adjustment on her part. When winter came, the Japanese POWs were sent to California, and German prisoners came to Camp McCoy. Lathrop was sharpening and sterilizing needles for serology when one of the POWs, who was sweeping the floor, offered, "I could do that." Realizing that would free her to perform other chores, Lathrop obtained the necessary permission. When the detainee was informed of his change of duty, he was so excited he threw his broom into the air—it turned out he was an orchestra conductor by profession. He and other prisoners entertained at a Christmas party given for resident WAACs by MPs.

Lathrop helped another POW who wanted to stay in America learn to read. "He *hated* his name, and with good reason," she laughs. "It was Adolph." POWs also worked as cooks in the mess hall.

One day, after a busy twenty-four-hour shift, Lathrop was relaxing on her bunk, listening to music and eating an apple. A friend came in and insisted she go out, going so far as to pull the curlers from the corporal's hair. Consequently, the pair went to a local hangout, where Lathrop sat down and ordered food. An inebriated comrade spotted her and staggered over, wanting to dance. Refusing to take "no" for an answer, he created an uncomfortable situation.

Don Lathrop, there to celebrate his separation from the Navy, came to her rescue. He approached her table, pretending to be her escort. Happy for the intervention, she responded, "Oh, there you are." He sat with her as she ate and then carried her back to camp in his Tin Lizzie. They became inseparable. He worked as driver for the hospital until her hitch ended and she returned to New Jersey. He followed her, but soon became homesick for the Badger State. Consequently, she agreed to be married in Wisconsin, prompting her parents to complain that she "robbed them of a Polish wedding." Nevertheless, her mother gave her the thousand dollars she had saved for Juilliard as a wedding present.

Don and Dusty Lathrop were married fifty years and produced eight children; two are deceased. As part of his job with Pioneer Telephone Company, the family lived in Wisconsin, Illinois, and Iowa, before being transferred to the Tar Heel state. "I fell in love with North Carolina when I was flying into Hickory and saw all those crape myrtles in bloom," recalls Lathrop. "I had never seen anything so beautiful, and everyone we met was good to us. But what I *really* loved was chicken and dumplings."

After Hickory, the telephone company transferred the Lathrops to Bethlehem, Jefferson, and eventually Madison, where Dusty has made her home for thirty-two years. Her husband passed away in 1996.

Frank Lauten

How in the world that ship held together, I'll never know.
Balls of fire came through the cracks of the ship.

"Hitler was rolling across Germany, taking one country right after the other," begins Frank Lauten. "I was in my last year of high school, working part-time at a grocery store, but I knew I would eventually be drafted. My ambition was to be a flying cadet. I applied to the Army Air Force and was given a date to appear at Douglas Airport in Charlotte, at 9:00 a.m. I was so excited I showed up at 7:00 a.m. and had to nap in the car until I was called for my appointment.

"I was doing fine until I was presented with several balls of variously colored yarn. That was when I learned that I am totally color-blind. I would never be a flying cadet." Pilots must be able to distinguish colors to recognize airport beacons, aircraft position lights, and chart symbols. Disappointed, Lauten returned to Madison to finish high school and accept a job with T. D. Meadow Grocery Company. As war raged on, he made one more unsuccessful attempt to enlist—this time in the Navy—before being drafted and sent to Camp Joseph T. Robinson in Arkansas.

Lauten was assigned to Tent 25, but before checking in, he took a walk around the camp area. When he finally reported to his tent, expecting to find some of his buddies waiting there, he was shocked to see Japanese inductees occupying every bunk. "Oh Lord," he muttered, "we've been invaded by Japan."

"Don't get excited," one of them said, laughing. "We're American-born Japanese; we're not going to hurt you." Lauten looks back on his association with these men warmly. He became especially close to one named Ito, whose son later judged the O. J. Simpson trial. Lauten witnessed firsthand the anguish of Japanese American soldiers training to fight for their country at the same time that their families were being herded into internment camps, the locations of which they were never told.

Lauten learned that on February 19, 1942, President Franklin D. Roosevelt signed Executive Order 9066, authorizing the roundup of 120,000 Japanese Americans, each of whom was then transported to one of ten internment camps located in California, Idaho, Utah, Arizona, Wyoming, Colorado, or Arkansas. More than two-thirds of those relocated were citizens of the United States.

According to a 1943 report issued by the War Relocation Authority, internees were forced to live in frame barracks covered with tarpaper, without plumbing or kitchen facilities of any type. Coal was scarce and blankets allotted sparingly. Food was meted out at the cost of forty-eight cents per person. In time, the government agreed that internees who enlisted in the United States Army could leave camp. The idea was not well received; only a small portion of the men chose to take advantage of the opportunity. Executive Order 9066 was rescinded in 1944. The last camp closed in 1945.

Lauten's greatest fear was that he would be assigned to the infantry after basic training. Ito, who worked in the orderly room and so had access to information regarding placement, approached him: "Lauten, you are the luckiest man I have ever seen. You and sixteen others are going to Orlando, Florida, to the Air Force." Lauten was ecstatic, although his happiness was tempered by the knowledge that his friend would never progress further than errand boy or some such menial position, due to his Japanese American heritage.

The airman was soon enjoying the sights of Orlando. He had never seen so many pretty girls in skimpy bathing suits. He remembers thinking,

"Good gracious, this is not the Air Force; this is Heaven." He changed his mind the next day, however, as he performed close order drills in the sweltering Florida heat.

He was working as an orderly clerk when he learned that three men were needed to attend electrical school in Chicago, Illinois. He sought and was awarded the opportunity. He was given seventy-five dollars a month for rent and food, and his daily responsibilities were limited to attending class seven hours and running around Grand Park once for exercise. "I was having a ball," he admits. "But I decided I had better get serious when I learned that those who flunked out of the school would be sent to the infantry." He subsequently passed with an eighty-five.

Lauten resumed his duties as orderly clerk at the Air Force Tactical Air Center in Orlando until he was tapped as one of two electrical school graduates to be sent to uptown Orlando to operate radio transmitters. "One day, I was informed that a transmitter had gotten off frequency while I was on duty, placing an airplane in jeopardy. The Pentagon was demanding an explanation. I pointed out that they had attempted to install FM equipment despite my warning that it would not maintain frequency due to the flat terrain. Apparently, the explanation was satisfactory; I received no disciplinary action." In time, a radio shack was built to house the transmitters.

Lauten was promoted to sergeant and put in charge of installing poles for FM transmitters to be spaced around the operations area. "At that particular time," he explains, "planes were tracked by human spotters, who reported to operators when planes passed particular locations. Things became much easier and more efficient when radar was installed."

The sergeant was in Orlando three years before being sent to Japan. En route to Okinawa, his ship passed Truk Island, a submarine base that remained under Japanese control. "When spotters identified an enemy periscope in the water, sailors ran to their battle stations and began firing." A battle ensued. "How in the world that ship held together, I'll never know," marvels Lauten. "Balls of fire came through the cracks of the ship. Somehow we prevailed, making it past the submarine and

Truk Island unscathed. In Okinawa, we were met with sniper fire from Japanese stragglers determined never to surrender."

Americans were housed in twelve-man tents—dimly lit due to a scarcity of light bulbs. "We heard the Seabees had a supply of bulbs, so my buddy and I *borrowed* a jeep and set out to get them," confesses Lauten. Not only did the light-bulb caper solve the lighting crisis, but the adventurous airmen also captured three Japanese soldiers in the process. They delivered their captives to the stockade and returned to camp to face yet another challenge.

Typhoon warnings had been issued, and rain was pouring through numerous holes in the tent. The men were advised to eat at their bunks, so Lauten opened a can of K-rations. "As I put the food to my mouth, something ran down my chin," he reflects. "I thought it was rain, but it was not rain—it was *blood*. I had split my finger wide open with that old can." He passed out, waking up to two burly GIs slapping him in the face and repeating his name. After applying a tourniquet to his finger, they supported him between them as they walked out into the 175 mile-per-hour winds. "We struggled forward and fell, got up and fell again, until we finally arrived at what we felt would be a safe haven from the storm—a Shinto Tomb.

"During another typhoon, the wind velocity was so great that we had to get down on the ground, hold onto each other's ankles, and crawl, snakelike, toward a Marine Quonset hut for safety. One man became so frightened, he turned loose of the heel he was holding and jumped into the cab of a nearby truck. A tent floor came flying through the air, crashed into the truck, and killed him instantly." The other men eventually wriggled their way to safety. "I lost everything I owned except the pair of cut-off jeans I was wearing," adds Lauten. Over the next couple of days, airplanes dropped food and clothing to the stranded men.

Lauten was taking a walk one Sunday when he came upon a gruesome sight: "At the mouth of one of the many caverns carved out under the mountains, I saw about five hundred bodies—women, children, and elderly. They had refused to leave their hiding places in the caves and were literally blown out with mortars." Later, he visited the site of what many consider to have been the most difficult battle fought by the US military during World War II—Bloody Nose Ridge (the Umurbrogol pocket). "I could see legs and arms of fallen soldiers sticking up in the air."

"We didn't have much to do on Okinawa; mainly, we tried to get Japanese holdouts to leave their caves," recalls Lauten. "Some came out at the promise of American cigarettes; others refused to surrender, fearing American domination more than starvation." The peace treaty had been signed, and the men wondered why they could not leave Okinawa. They wrote letters to their congressmen, asking to be allowed to return to the states. After what seemed an eternity, they boarded a ship for Seattle, Washington. From there, Lauten traveled to Fort Bragg to receive his discharge and then home to Madison.

Lauten and his uncle, Carl Lauten, together owned and operated the local Ford dealership in Madison. Martha Moring, a young Woman's College graduate from Greensboro, had been hired to work with the Rockingham County Welfare Department. She occasionally brought her 1940 model Ford to the dealership for minor repairs. "I got up my nerve and asked her for a date," he confides. She refused. "I got up my nerve twice more and received the same answer."

One day, Martha called Lauten to ask for help. She had been on Mayodan Mountain delivering potatoes to a family when she was involved in an automobile accident. Her car would not start, and potatoes were strewn all over the road. He hurried to her aid, picked up dozens of potatoes, and loaned her his car, and a relationship was born. He smiles as he recalls, "That little old bag of potatoes bought me fifty-five years of pure grace and three of the finest children you'll ever want to find—Jan, Conrad, and Bill."

Martha Lauten died December 20, 2003. Lauten continues to live in the family home and is active in church and community affairs.

James "Radio" Lawson

I saw a lot of men killed when they tried to leave the LCVP; others fell as they raced toward the beach, and barbed-wire traps and mines planted in the water claimed even more.

Sarah Lawson wipes a tear as she shares memories and photographs of her late husband, James "Radio" Lawson: one picture depicts Lawson as a young sailor in World War II, during the time he participated in landings on Omaha, Utah, Iwo Jima, and Okinawa; another shows him with sons Bob and Bill, who lost their mother— Lawson's first wife—when they were two and five. Finally, there is an image of him standing beside a moonshine still he raided while he was a deputy sheriff with the Rockingham County Sheriff's Department.

Lawson completed sixth grade before dropping out of school to help on the family farm. In 1943, the nineteen-year-old received his draft notice. "I wanted to go into the Marines," he confesses, "but I was appointed to the Navy instead. After I saw what happened to the Marines on Iwo Jima and Okinawa, I figured it was a good thing I didn't get in." He was sent to Bainbridge, Maryland, for boot camp. There he marched, practiced firing weapons and identifying air and sea crafts, and qualified in swimming. He learned to tie knots in the legs of his bell-bottom trousers to create an emergency life preserver.

"After a seven-day leave at Christmas, I was transferred to Little Creek, Virginia, and later to Fort Pierce, Florida, to undergo amphibious training in warm, choppy waters," explains Lawson. He was assigned to an LCVP, a landing craft built to operate effectively in the surf. It could pull away from the beach and turn in its own length. Designed to land men, equipment, and/or cargo on the beach, it could carry thirty-six men or four men and a jeep. Four seamen operated the diminutive vessel, without which the Allies never could have landed over open beaches. "We rotated duties as coxswain, hookman, signalman, and gunner."

"From Fort Pierce, I traveled to Pier 92 in New York City, to join the crew of the USS *Thurston*, the transport ship that would be both home and duty station for the next three years," says Lawson. "On March 10, 1944, we sailed for Cardiff, England, where we trained for the Omaha Beach landing scheduled June 5—D-day." On that date, however, the waters were too boisterous to carry out the mission. They would have to wait an additional day.

At 0800 on July 6, the men hit the water, with feisty Lawson at the helm of the landing ship. Battling his way through ten- and twelve-foot waves, he delivered his load of soldiers to the beach: "I saw a lot of men killed when they tried to leave the LCVP; others fell as they raced toward the beach, and barbed-wire traps and mines planted in the water claimed even more." Soon, virile, well-honed bodies were reduced to an array of bloody fragments and stumps scattered across the sand. Shaken, Lawson rewound the ramp to the vehicle and backed away from the massacre.

"It took us about two hours to make it back to the *Thurston*, anchored eleven miles out to sea. We picked up another load of soldiers and headed out again, this time for Utah Beach." The sea had quieted down somewhat as the day progressed, but Lawson saw little difference in the reception troops received there and the one they had received on Omaha: "It was the same," he laments. "There were a lot of dead soldiers." He tells of seeing the paratroopers who had been dropped earlier to secure the main road and cause general chaos. After the last man disembarked, the LCVP returned to the ship and was loaded aboard.

The *Thurston* returned to Weymouth, England. "For a while we ran up and down the coastline delivering troops to various locations: Scotland, North Africa, Italy, France, the Panama Canal." Eventually, they returned to the states, where Lawson enjoyed a seven-day leave before sailing for Pearl Harbor, Hawaii, and on to Saipan in the Marianna Islands. "Saipan had been captured by Allied forces and was being used for training before the invasion of Iwo Jima," he points out.

"We transported Marines to Iwo Jima on February 19, 1945. I shuttled them to the beach in the LCVP." The volcanic island was heavily fortified with bunkers, hidden artillery, and eleven miles of underground tunnels. Japanese soldiers allowed the GIs to come ashore before blasting them with machine gun and artillery fire. Some of the fiercest fighting of the Pacific War followed, with the Marines sustaining devastating losses. Adding to the bloodbath were the kamikaze pilots, who made repeated assaults on the amphibious forces storming the beachhead. Lawson's voice fills with emotion as he stresses, "I carried survivors of those suicide attacks back to the ship for treatment. And when the American flag was raised on Mount Suribachi four days after the initial invasion, I saluted it from the deck of the *Thurston*" (Radio Lawson. Interview. June 13, 2002).

On April 9, 1945, the *Thurston* arrived in Okinawa, where the largest amphibious assault in the Pacific Theater was already underway. "I unloaded Marines on the beach for what would be the bloodiest battle of the Pacific War," he declares. One hundred thousand frantic Japanese warriors dug into caves or tunnels and fought furiously to hold this important island—just 340 miles from mainland Japan. Hundreds of kamikaze pilots sank 34 American crafts and damaged 368 others. More than 38,000 Americans were wounded, with 12,000 killed or missing in action. The 82-day-long battle lasted from early April through mid-June ("Battle of Okinawa").

While hostilities raged on Okinawa, troops on the *Thurston* received two important notifications: first, on April 12, their commander-in-chief, President Franklin D. Roosevelt died, and second, on May 8, the conflict in Europe ended. War in the Pacific came to a dramatic climax when atomic bombs fell on Hiroshima (August 6) and Nagasaki (August 9). Japan surrendered unconditionally aboard the USS *Missouri* on

September 2, 1945. "We helped transport troops from their stations of deployment to the states," notes Lawson, obviously grateful for a happy mission.

In April 1946, Lawson was given $300 in mustering-out pay and was honorably discharged from the Navy. He came home and farmed a couple of years before going to work for Madison Grocery. After joining the Rockingham County Sheriff's Department on February 1, 1957, he gained a reputation for hunting down and destroying moonshine stills. "I could just smell 'em out," he told friends. He stayed with the department for twenty-two years but was dismissed—five months prior to gaining full retirement benefits—when a new sheriff was elected. He then worked with the Madison Police Department for fifteen years.

He married his second wife, the former Sarah Hopper, on April 22, 1962. Sarah, who could not bear children, embraced her stepsons as her own. "I did everything for them except change their diapers," she boasts.

James "Radio" Lawson died on May 13, 2005.

James "Big Jim" Louden

*The B-26 Marauder did only one thing on
one engine, and that was go down.*

June 6, 1944: Second Lieutenant James "Big Jim" Louden awoke at 3:00 a.m. to hear Brigadier General Fred Anderson announce that thousands of American troops would be landing on Normandy at 6:30 a.m.; bombs should be dropped at precisely 6:25 a.m. to clear Utah Beach of German mines and other obstructions. Louden, along with thirty-five other pilots in his group, took off that morning in the pouring rain, despite having been briefed that they had to fly *below* the clouds no matter what the altitude: it was imperative that they see their target clearly. There were 5,500 ships in the channel—a bridge of vessels from England to France. Eleven thousand Allied aircraft dotted the sky. Louden remembers thinking, "Here I am a twenty-three-year-old kid, and I am seeing the greatest show on earth; the greatest show of the century, and I have a front-row seat."

The weather had cleared somewhat by the time the pilots reached the beach. There was a cloud layer about thirty thousand feet above ground. They flew underneath it to drop their bombs, hitting their target at exactly 6:25 a.m. "Out of the corner of my eye, I could see the first troops getting out of their landing crafts and wading ashore," he says. "But it would be days before I would learn how successful the mission had been. Army losses at Utah Beach were minimal; it has been recognized as one of the greatest exhibitions of coordination between the Army, Navy, Air Force, and Marines ever seen."

After Louden's group dropped their bombs that morning, they returned to base, reloaded their aircraft with five-hundred-pound bombs, grabbed sandwiches, refueled their airplanes, and flew back to France. Their orders were to bomb a German marshalling railroad yard and transportation depot near the city of Saint-Lô. Despite the "flak" that was exploding all about them, they hit their target. "I was glad to finally get the bombardier's signal that it was okay to turn around and head for home," he confesses. "Two missions on D-day were enough for me. That was quite a day."

His bomb group, the 397th, became known as the "Bridge Busters" because they supported General George S. Patton's drive from Normandy to Berlin by blowing up bridges, allowing retreating German troops to be captured. On one occasion, after blowing up the Rhine River Bridge in Cologne, Germany, Louden took a direct burst of flak in his right engine. He would have to make it all the way back to England on one engine. "The B-26 Marauder did only one thing on one engine, and that was *go down*." Instructing his crew to throw out everything possible and put on parachutes in case they had to bail out over the English Channel, he headed for Manson Emergency Landing Strip on the White Cliffs of Dover, built especially for crippled Allied aircraft returning from Germany. "We made it, and as a result, one of my favorite songs has always been 'The White Cliffs of Dover.'"

Over the next two years, Louden experienced a number of life-changing events in rapid succession: on February 9, 1945, he was promoted to captain; seventeen days later (February 26), he was awarded the Distinguished Flying Cross. Shortly thereafter, on May 8, 1945, Germany surrendered, bringing an end to the war in Europe. The captain was discharged from the Army on November 15, 1945, though he remained in the reserves.

On the following December 15, he married Peggy Neuner in a Lutheran church in Pittsburgh, Pennsylvania, and settled in to sell meat products for the St. Louis Independent Packing Company. Much to Peggy's dismay, however, in February 1946, her husband received a letter from the War Department, offering him an opportunity to qualify for a regular commission in the Army Air Corps, which he enthusiastically accepted. On June 28, 1946, he received word that he was again on active duty—this time as a second lieutenant.

Louden was assigned to the Forty-Seventh Bomb Group, an A-26 light bomber night attack group stationed at Biggs Air Force Base in El Paso, Texas. In November 1948, the group took delivery of the first four-engine jet aircraft to fly in the United States—the B-45 jet bomber. As a result, the group was transferred to Barksdale Air Force Base in Shreveport, Louisiana, where they would have access to a longer runway. "In 1949, I was asked to serve as public relations officer for the bomb group. I promoted a contest to select a name for the new airplane; *Tornado* was chosen. I also made two nationwide public relations broadcasts from the cockpit of the B-45 from forty-five thousand feet in the air." Both flights were successful.

On June 9, 1949, Captain Louden and Captain Ralph Smith were scheduled to learn to fly the B-45. They, along with instructor pilot, Captain Milton Costello, headed for the landing strip at about 10:30 a.m. They tossed a coin to determine which of the two learner pilots would be first to practice flying the aircraft. Louden lost. "I crawled into the navigator's compartment in the nose of the airplane, where I stayed for the next two hours while Captain Smith practiced stalling, pulling out of stalls, taking off, and landing."

The time came for the captains to exchange seats so that Louden could take his turn flying the B-45. As Smith was coming in for his last landing—about four miles short of the runway on the final approach, full wing flaps down—suddenly the torque tube that drove the wing flap on the right side broke, causing the right wing flap to snap up. With the right wing flap up and the left down, the airplane began to roll. "We were about two thousand feet above ground," declares Louden. "Costello grabbed the controls and tried to pull the wing up by applying full power to all four engines. He failed."

When they hit the ground, traveling about three hundred miles per hour, sixteen thousand pounds of jet fuel exploded. Smith and Costello were "blown into a million pieces." Louden, separated from the others by a five-inch firewall, was thrown 150 yards from the impact point into a clump of trees by a creek bank.

Jim Sharpe, an Air Force supply sergeant, found Louden's crash helmet—dented and marked with a six-inch gash. Shortly thereafter, Ned Touchstone found the unconscious pilot hanging from the limb of a nearby tree, his left arm bleeding profusely. Touchstone took off his T-shirt and made a tourniquet. The captain had a broken back, broken legs, cerebral concussion, and multiple injuries, including first and second-degree burns. Peggy Louden, visiting in Pittsburgh, was notified by the commanding officer at Barksdale that she should come immediately; her husband was "gravely ill." Peggy sat beside her husband's bed daily for the next two and a half years.

Louden remained in a coma for seventeen days, and even after waking up, he drifted in and out of coherency for some time. A four-star general, assigned to a training command at Barksdale, came every day to check on the pilot's progress. During one visit, Louden fancied him to be the former manager of the New York Giants. Turning to Peggy, he commented, "Here is Muggsy McGraw, come to sign me up for a major league contract." Eventually, his head cleared, and according to the colonel, he "has been fairly normal ever since."

Big Jim wanted to fly again—and fly he did. Following extensive therapy at Walter Reed Army Medical Center in Washington, DC, he rejoined the Forty-Seventh Bomb Group at Langley Air Force Base in Norfolk, Virginia, as public relations officer. On April Fools' Day, 1951, he fooled everyone by being pronounced physically fit to return to the skies. Later that same year, he was promoted to major. During the Korean Conflict (1952), Major Louden flew troops and supplies into Korea and flew wounded soldiers out, delivering them to a station hospital in Nagoya, Japan. A busy decade later (March 1961), he obtained the rank of lieutenant colonel.

In 1968, he volunteered to undertake a top-secret operation in Vietnam: every other day for ninety days, he flew his C-130—unescorted—over Laos, taping the conversations of the Viet Cong with radar equipment. After each ten-hour flight, he flew to DaNang to deliver the tapes before returning to Cam Ranh Bay. War strategists decoded and interpreted the recordings to help them determine how to conduct the war the following day.

Louden interrupts his story to lean back in his chair and sip his drink. This gives me an opportunity to examine the sports and aviation mementos that dominate his living room: plaques, awards, letters, and commendations obscure one wall; books, magazines, pamphlets, pictures, and models compete for space on tabletops and snake along the carpet, caressing furniture and baseboards. Noting my interest in his memorabilia, he shares a bit of philosophy: "Yesterday is a canceled check, tomorrow is a promissory note, and every day begins a new chapter."

After God and family, Louden's great loves are baseball and airplanes. By the tender age of eight, he had already decided that he would be either a pilot or a major league baseball player. When he was sixteen, living in a small community just outside Pittsburgh, his baseball manager convinced him to try out for the Pittsburgh Pirates. The six-foot-two first baseman, known for hitting homeruns, traveled the short distance to Forbes Field, where he was one of four hundred seeking a major league contract. "I made it through five days before being cut," he assures me. "Only six made the team, and I wasn't one of them."

With that door closed, Louden focused on his other passion—flying. At eighteen, he walked into the recruiting office in downtown Pittsburgh and asked if there was an opening *somewhere* where he could enlist and apply for pilot training. Told that such an opportunity existed at Lowry Field in Denver, Colorado, he exclaimed, "Wonderful. Give me the paperwork." Unfortunately, he needed parental consent, and his father refused to sign. Determined, he waited until he was twenty-one, marched into the same recruiting office, and joined the United States Army.

Following thirteen weeks of basic training in Fort Lee, Virginia, Louden applied for pilot education. He was required to appear before a board of officers and complete a battery of physical and mental tests—all of which he passed easily. In October 1942, he was assigned to Kelly Field in San Antonio, Texas, to undergo a year of pilot instruction. On July 29, 1943, at Ellington Field in Houston, he received his wings and was promoted to second lieutenant in the Army Air Corps.

After pilot school, the second lieutenant went to Del Rio, Texas, to learn to fly the Martin Marauder B-26, a medium-range bomber, and from there to MacDill Air Force Base in Florida to join the 397th Medium Range Bomb group. In early 1944, he sailed from New York City to Greenock, Scotland, and on to Braintree—ninety miles east of London—where he was assigned a crew. On April 1, 1944, he flew the first of 650 hours of air combat.

A quarter of a century later, on April 1, 1979, Lieutenant Colonel Louden, fifty, retired from the US Air Force and joined Peggy and their two children, James Jr. and Teri, in Fayetteville. He had served his country continuously for almost thirty years. Unable to sit and do nothing, he sold real estate for the next fifteen years. In 1993, he lost his beloved Peggy, and in 2002, he moved into the Masonic and Eastern Star Retirement Home in Greensboro. There he continues his long-standing practice of performing volunteer services—this time in the neurosurgery department of Moses Cone Hospital, directing visitors to patients' rooms and providing support for concerned family members.

Orville Mabe

I thought to the Lord I would never make
nine months in the trenches.

"**R**ounds were hitting so close that dirt fell in all around us in the bunker," recalls Orville Mabe as he describes his first hours on the Korean front. After landing in Pusan in the dead of night, he was shuttled onto a train and rushed to the front line. Warned to expect shooting, he glanced about him in the car, fixating on the windows: *What happened to the glass?* he wondered. *Shot out*, he decided, just as all forms of light were being extinguished.

Placed in an eight-by-ten, sandbag-lined bunker, the untested rifleman had no idea where he was or from which direction the enemy was advancing. Artillery and napalm exploded, lighting the dark sky like elaborate fireworks, the accompanying din such that Mabe subsequently sustained permanent hearing loss. "Planes were coming so fast and low," he says. "You couldn't hear them until they were on top of you."

Second Battalion Fox Company entered the campaign as peace talks generated a shift in tactics from huge offensives and withdrawals to protection of main lines of resistance. This approach consisted of building bunkers, laying wire, and patrolling. Massive artillery battles replaced small arms encounters. Intensity of combat matched the ebb and flow of hopes for truce, as negotiations droned on over details as seemingly benign as the shape of the table.

The company's approximately two hundred men scattered up and down the front line awaiting the inevitable attacks, which usually came in late evening. Sometimes patrols of eight to ten soldiers were sent out to make contact with the enemy. As men fell, they were carried back to the relative safety of the trenches. "One fell, and we didn't see him; he lay out there all night, which violated our creed. The next night, a patrol went and got him while the rest of us fired cover."

"We took turns guarding the trenches," remembers Mabe, who hated standing the eight-hour shifts in subzero weather. "If anyone tells you he was not afraid, he is lying. It was so dark I couldn't see a piece of white paper in front of my eyes. Instead of my rifle, I held a forty-five pistol with the safety off. Sometimes I'd get a feeling someone was there. I'd feel all around me with that forty-five: if I had touched anything, I would have fired."

Weary warriors carried out their duties wearing big parkas with fur-lined hoods. They melted snow for drinking water but sometimes went thirty days without a bath. Medics placed medicine packets in their mouths to keep them from freezing, and C-rations were carried next to soldiers' bodies for warmth. During the first winter in Korea, 5,300 Americans—including Mabe—suffered frostbite.

"I saw a little action," offers Mabe, who grew up in Sandy Ridge and graduated Stokes High School before receiving his draft notice on October 10, 1951. After basic training at Fort Riley, Kansas, he went to Seattle, Washington, and trained in the operation of firearms, a specialty he put to good use as leader of a heavy weapons squad in the frozen tundra of North Korea. He "saw a little action" on such bloody battlefields as Old Baldy—also known as Suicide Hill—where Communist causalities exceeded one thousand, and at Arrowhead Ridge, where General Fry marveled that the preparatory fire was "beyond anything I have known in my previous considerable military experience."

He also "saw a little action" on October 10, 1952, when his battalion effectively carried out a raiding mission on Chinese strongholds at T-bone Ridge to divert enemy fire from beleaguered White Horse Mountain, which changed from Communist to American hands twenty-four times. In November, he "saw a little action" when he helped repel repeated enemy probes on Alligator Jaws and Porkchop Hill, where frantic GIs shot themselves rather than endure the carnage enveloping them.

Contrary to his initial fear that he would "not make nine months in the trenches," when Mabe finally accumulated enough points to return to the states, he had survived eleven months. Sadly, he and his comrades were unaware, as they risked their lives to interrupt the spread of communism, that they were being largely ignored by the news media in their own country—so much so that the Korean Conflict became known as the Forgotten War. In three years, fifty-eight thousand Americans lost their lives in what was labeled a "police action," although it featured some of the most intense fighting ever experienced by US forces, as well as some of the worst combat conditions.

The exhausted corporal was sent to Camp Rucker, Alabama, to await discharge three months later. While there, he purchased a brand new Bel Air Chevrolet, a trophy he suspects is what first attracted the attention of Gracie Moore, a pretty brunette from his hometown who became his wife in 1956.

After their marriage, the Mabes relocated to Rockingham County, where Gracie worked with Washington Mills and he with Madison Throwing. The couple has two sons, Timothy and Michael.

Thomas McCollum

Patton was rough and tough, but he treated us well.

T hings moved rapidly for Thomas McCollum of Madison after
he was drafted. He went first to Camp Croft, South Carolina;
then to Fort Bragg, North Carolina; Fort McClellan, Alabama;
Fort Meade, Maryland; and finally Camp Kilmer, New Jersey, before
boarding the *Queen Mary* to cross the Atlantic Ocean. He sailed to
Glasgow, Scotland, and took a train from there to Weymouth, England,
where he boarded a boat for what he calls "the worst ride of my life,"
terminating at LaHavre, France. A short time later, he joined the 102nd
Infantry Division at Lenox, Germany.

McCollum and his companions were scheduled to cross the Ruhr
River in early February 1945, but the Germans had blown up a dam—
flooding the area and delaying their crossing until the end of the month.
Two days later, they were advancing across an open area, taking small
arms fire, when McCollum felt a sharp pang in his right leg. He fell to
the ground, realizing he had been hit. "A medic patched me up, but I lay
there for what seemed like an eternity. I thought I was going to have to
spend the night out there."

Eventually, one of the soldiers in his unit came by, escorting four
German prisoners. "He carried them to where they were supposed to
be," recalls McCollum. "But it wasn't long before he came back with
those same four German prisoners. They put me on a stretcher, and those
prisoners carried me to the first aid station." The next day, McCollum
went to Arken, Germany, for further aid and to await transportation

to General Hospital in Belgium, where he remained until he was well enough to rejoin his unit.

The war in Europe was winding down—the Germans in retreat. McCollum and his team were charged with clearing out towns and villages, making sure everything was secure. "The civilians were glad to see us," he says. "We took enemy soldiers we found hiding in homes and buildings, but we left the civilians alone."

The division crossed the Rhine River without incident. On their drive to the Elbe River, they came across an abandoned concentration camp. The prisoners had been removed, but the soldiers discovered two cremation furnaces, along with a mass grave—fifty feet long by ten feet wide. "They left people's legs sticking out. It was inhuman," decries McCollum, shaking his head. When the soldiers finally arrived at the Elbe, their instructions were to wait there until the Russians arrived. "The only activity we saw during that time was German civilians and soldiers crossing the river to get into American hands. They did *not* want to be taken by the Russians."

The war in Europe ended on May 8, 1945. McCollum says that his division had captured 86 towns and more than 145,000 German prisoners of war. They had lost in excess of 1,000 men; almost 4,000 had been wounded; and 564 had been captured by the enemy or were missing in action. McCollum, accompanied by nine enlisted men and one officer, escorted a trainload of displaced persons, previously captured by the Germans, to Yugoslavia.

McCollum could have been ordered to join the war in the Pacific, which was still raging, but instead he became part of the occupation forces in Europe. One day, he was told to report immediately to Regimental Headquarters. Not knowing what to expect, he commented to his captain, "I don't know whether I want to go or not."

His captain replied, "If you really don't want to go, I can stop it. But to tell you the truth, it will probably be a break for you."

It turned out that the captain was right. McCollum had been chosen to attend a clerical school outside of Paris, France. From there, he was sent to Frankfurt, Germany—Supreme Headquarters for Allied forces in Europe. His assignment was to assist in documenting the history of the Allied forces in Europe during World War II by typing the notes of General George S. Patton and other officers.

"The work was done in a resort town just outside Frankfurt, which for the most part had been spared the devastation of war. While we were there, we lived like royalty. We stayed in a hotel staffed with maid service; our meals were served on dining tables covered with linen cloths, set with fine china and silverware. A live band entertained while we ate."

On December 9, 1945, one day before he was scheduled to return to the states, General Patton was involved in an automobile accident while on a day trip to hunt pheasant near Mannheim. He died on December 21 at the military hospital in Heidelberg. "Patton was rough and tough," admits McCollum, "but he treated us well."

McCollum was ordered back to Frankfurt, where he was assigned to the message center. All correspondence to and from Europe, both routine and classified, came through his office. He remained there for the remainder of his military tenure. In June 1946, the twenty-one-year-old corporal sailed for home, having earned the following medals: Purple Heart, Bronze Star, Occupation Ribbon, European Theatre of Operation with two Bronze Stars, Combat Infantry Badge, Good Conduct Medal, Combat Infantry Badge, Victory Medal, and Army Commendation Ribbon.

McCollum is married to the former Marion Tucker. They have three sons: Tommy, Denny, and Michael. Before retiring, he was employed by McCollum Motor Company, Farmers Supply, and finally Rockingham County Department of Transportation.

John McGlohon

There was a brilliant flash directly below our plane ... as if someone had fired a big flashbulb directly in our eyes.

T he first time I saw John McGlohon, he was standing in his front yard waving furiously toward his house. His fellow veteran, Pete Comer, and I had traveled the short distance from Madison to Asheboro and had been driving up and down the street looking for the correct house number. John came to greet us—old friend and new—with smiles and hugs. At that moment, I realized that there are no strangers in John McGlohon's world. I was not surprised to learn that, after retiring from the military, he not only served his community for thirty years as fireman but also served sixteen as city councilman and two as mayor pro tem.

He invited us into his home, introduced us to his wife of sixty years, showed us pictures of his sons, Steve and Bob, and offered us refreshments. Only then did he settle back in his chair and begin to relate the story that we had come to hear, one that he has repeated often through the years.

"When I joined the Army Air Corps in June of 1941, I was handed a ticket to Montgomery, Alabama, and placed on a southbound train. I arrived at the depot in Montgomery at 2:00 a.m. and was met by a soldier driving a two-and-a-half-ton Army truck. Riding alone in the back of that truck, I made my first appearance at Maxwell Field. I was issued a mattress cover, mess kit, and cot, and directed to place the cot 'anywhere I liked' in the empty aircraft hanger—my home for the next several days. Within the week, the hanger swarmed with identical cots as new recruits arrived. The following week, we were all moved to a tent city to begin basic training."

Hearing that a combat unit was being organized on base, McGlohon requested transfer into the group. Consequently, he became a member of the Third Photo Mapping Squadron, which gathered aerial photographs to be used in producing detailed military maps. He was assigned to the orderly room where administrative tasks were performed. On each side of the orderly room were darkrooms used for developing and printing. He loved to go into the darkrooms and watch the men work. Unfortunately, once he was in one of the rooms, he could not leave until the film was developed. Quite often, when needed in the orderly room, he was locked in a darkroom. Eventually, someone else was assigned his clerical responsibilities, and he was trained in photography.

For his efforts, McGlohon earned twenty-one dollars per month. Of that amount, he sent seven dollars home, had seven taken out for PX checks, and kept seven to spend. On Sunday, December 7, 1941, he used a nickel to ride the bus to town, attended church, paid a dime to get into a movie, spent a nickel on popcorn, and saved five cents to get back to base. "As I was enjoying the movie," he recalls, "a man suddenly walked onto the stage and announced, 'All military personnel are to report to base immediately; Pearl Harbor has been bombed.' From that minute on, we were on a wartime footing, and everything changed greatly."

The squadron moved to MacDill Air Force Base in Tampa, Florida, on December 27. They built two-story barracks for housing and a photo lab for their own use, although they also operated the base photo lab. McGlohon continues, "In the fall of 1942, Sergeant Jim Allen and I were assigned to go on our first out-of-country mission to South America. We were to be lab techs and, once at our station, build and operate a photo lab to develop and print film taken by our flight crews. I never knew who had the nerve to pick two nineteen-year-old kids to take on this job, but it was great."

The afternoon they were preparing to leave MacDill Field, the lead plane, piloted by the squadron commander and carrying both the engineering officer and the first sergeant, crashed on takeoff, killing all on board. The remaining members of the mission left a few days later, and after a bit of island hopping en route to South America, they reached their final destination—Recife, Brazil.

McGlohon and Allen built their photo lab. He explains, "We would develop the film, make a set of prints, and send them to Tampa on the next plane going up. We would send the film up only after we knew for sure that the prints had arrived safely. Most of the flights involved mapping the coast of Brazil and the upper regions of the Amazon River over rain forests, as far as the eye could see. When Sergeant Cain, one of our photographers, became ill and had to return to the states, I was given his plane and started flying photo missions."

Eventually, McGlohon's squadron was brought back to the states for reassignment. This time, they headed north: after making stops in New York, Illinois, Wisconsin, and Montana, they flew to Canada's British Columbia and the Yukon Territory, mapping what would become the Alaskan Highway as they went. They stayed several days in Anchorage, Alaska, before reaching their final base at the little Indian village of Naknek. They lived in Quonset huts, while the planes remained outside in the cold. The supply ship had been iced-in about two miles offshore, so until the ice was thick enough to allow a truck to get to the supply ship, they sent out hunting and fishing details to search for food.

Their main mission was to do aerial reconnaissance of the islands of Kiska and Attu, where Japanese troops were gathered and a battle was expected. McGlohon's group covered the invasion fleet in the harbor at Cold Bay and the area around Dutch Harbor. After the Japanese had been removed, they mapped all of Alaska and western Canada. When the mission was completed, they returned to the United States.

On McGlohon's first night back at MacDill, he received word that his brother, an officer and bombardier, was in Tampa but was shipping out the following morning. McGlohon took a taxi to the railroad station and found his brother just in time to walk with him along the tracks as he was leaving. It was the last time the two would see each other. His brother's plane crashed in England, killing all aboard except one gunner.

In 1943, McGlohon's crew was ordered to the China-Burma-India Theater to map the eastern end of the Himalayan Mountains (the Hump) and the area of the Lido Road in Burma. They flew from Florida to Natal, Brazil, and from there, they headed east across the Atlantic Ocean. Their first stop was the Ascension Islands—landing among the birds. From there they flew to Africa and on to India. Their assigned base was in the village of Guskara, India, but they mostly flew out of the British fields in the Assam Valley.

"We carried extra bomb bay tanks of fuel and had five-gallon jerry tanks on all available space in the plane. We would fly through the mountains and land at Kunming, China, where we would unload some of the fuel for the Flying Tigers. With the reduced weight, we could make our return trip at an elevation needed for mapping the Hump," declares McGlohon, who about this time contracted malaria and was sent to Ondal for treatment. He recovered nicely and rejoined his squadron in time to complete their mission before returning to the states.

At Smoky Hill Air Force Base in Salina, Kansas, McGlohon served with Gunnery Sergeant Wilbert "Stocky" Stockdale and Navigator Lieutenant Mac Hyman. After the war, Hyman wrote *No Time for Sergeants*, basing his main character on Stockdale. The book was made into a movie starring Andy Griffith.

In the fall of 1944, McGlohon was reassigned to Flight C of the First Photo Reconnaissance Squadron and sent back to the China-Burma-India Theater. While there, members of his crew were awarded the Distinguished Flying Cross and the Air Medal for discovering what became known as the jet stream. They were on a mission to Mukden, Manchuria. McGlohon describes the incident:

"As we were attempting our approach into the target area, I watched a spot on my viewfinder which should have indicated our air speed. However, I noticed that the spot wasn't moving. After timing it for several minutes, I called the pilot and advised him we were not moving. We were facing winds that were traveling as fast in one direction as we were *supposed* to be traveling in the other, and it was just a standoff." McGlohon believes that this was the first time the US Air Force had encountered this phenomenon. They had to abort the mission and return to base because they had expended too much fuel.

In 1945, the group was ordered to leave China and rejoin the Third Photo Squadron on the Island of Guam. McGlohon always carried a pass, signed by General Hap Arnold, authorizing him to photograph anything he saw. He says, "On the morning of August 6, 1945, we found ourselves over the home islands on what we felt was a routine mission. But just before 0830, as we approached the city of Hiroshima, Eddie Laurie, in the right blister, called over the intercom to say that he had just seen a B-29 headed in the opposite direction, as if it was headed to the island of Iwo Jima—and a possible emergency landing.

"Within seconds of Eddie calling our attention to the plane, there was a brilliant flash directly below our plane. The light was as if someone had fired a big flashbulb directly in our eyes. Our pilots and gunners really caught the full blast from the flash. My only vision was through a twelve-inch-square glass below my viewfinder, so I did not get the same effect as other crew members.

"Not knowing what caused this bright light, we assumed that the plane we had just seen had salvoed his bomb load and gotten a good hit on an ammunition dump or an oil tank. We wanted to give the crew credit for the job they had done. I reached over and turned on my intervalometer, which controlled my cameras, and took photographs as we flew directly over the upcoming cloud. I picked up a K-20 handheld camera, walked up into the blister, and took other photos as we flew from the scene, still unaware of what we had photographed."

The team arrived back on Guam around 4:00 p.m., loaded their film on a truck, and headed for the lab. When they arrived, they were surprised to find Marine guards posted at the door; they had to get permission to enter the building and unload their film. "In the lab I noticed that Sergeant Johnny Dornblazer was running film across a plotting board, and on one of the nine-by-nine negatives, there was a small photo of the cloud that I had photographed that morning. The cloud on Dornblazer's negative was very small, only about an inch high—the negative having been taken from another plane miles away, using a long focal length lens."

Asked what the picture represented, Dornblazer replied that it was an atomic bomb. McGlohon told him that he had taken pictures of it that morning and that this was the first idea he had of what he had photographed. No one believed him. They argued that if his crew had been that close to an atomic bomb, they would probably all be dead by morning. They were checked with Geiger counters, and their plane was moved to the end of the runway to be inspected for contamination: all tested clean. Only after they dug out their film and had it processed were they taken seriously. Still, the McGlohon account was not included in the historical data, and his photograph was credited to another.

When the second atomic bomb was dropped on August 9, 1945, the crew suspected that the end of the war was in sight. Japan surrendered in the harbor at Tokyo on September 2, and suddenly, the Air Force was faced with letting go of unneeded personnel. Having accumulated the second largest number of points, McGlohon was one of the first to leave.

The technical sergeant caught a flight to California. From there, he traveled by train to Fort Bragg, where he was processed for discharge and awarded his Ruptured Duck. He hitched a ride to Asheboro, slipping into his home a little after dark. He asked his surprised parents if they "fed anyone who didn't have a ration card."

In 1995, at a forty-year reunion of his photo squadron, McGlohon got his first glimpse of the photo he had taken the morning the atomic bomb was dropped on Hiroshima. Elmer Dixon, the squadron's lab chief had saved a copy. It was dated August 6, 1945, and marked "SECRET."

The following account appeared in the *Charlotte Observer* on August 1, 2010:

> Ken Samuelson has spent the past two years researching and
> vindicating McGlohon's claim. "He was there. The plane
> was there. There is no question," says Samuelson ...

Here is what he found: Before the bombing, an order was issued to the 20th Air Force barring its planes from flying within 50 miles of Hiroshima the morning of August 6. McGlohon's unit, now under the 8th Air Force, was not on the distribution list. Samuelson has a copy of the order.

He also has a copy of the flight's mission report, indicating the route McGlohon's plane traveled that day and noting the rising cloud the crew had seen.

At the moment the bomb exploded, McGlohon and his crew were approaching Hiroshima at about 27,000 feet and flying at at least 275 mph. They would have passed over the city before the mushroom cloud had time to reach their altitude, Samuelson says ...

The film McGlohon delivered to the lab was commingled with film from the Enola Gay's reconnaissance plane and other photo planes later sent toward Hiroshima. Because McGlohon's plane wasn't supposed to be in the area, lab techs would not have known he took the picture. It is credited to a 20th Air Force plane that was actually miles away at the time. (Quillin)

Retired officer Clarence Becker, operations officer for the Third Photo Squadron, corroborates McGlohon's report, confirming that he sent them out that day, not knowing that there was going to be an atomic bomb drop.

The Historic Aviation Memorial Museum in Tyler, Texas, now displays McGlohon's photo, the only one that looks straight down at the mushroom cloud.

Colonel James "Big Jim" Louden. *Courtesy Pete Comer*

Combat Airmen/Joshua's Troops. *Courtesy Pete Comer*

Olga "Dusty" Lathrop. *Courtesy Olga Lathrop*

Members of original Combat Airmen/Joshua's Troops board. *Courtesy Pete Comer*

Pansy Collins at the Rockingham County Veterans Memorial. *Courtesy Pete Comer*

Pansy Collins Funeral Truck. *Courtesy Pete Comer*

A-Bomb cloud over Hiroshima filmed by John McGlohon (8-6-1945). *Courtesy Pete Comer*

John McGlohon and camera. *Courtesy John McGlohon*

Bob Comer. *Courtesy Pete Comer*

Pete Comer photographs Malmedy Massacre Trial. *Courtesy Pete Comer*

Lee Donald Tuttle. *Courtesy Lee Tuttle*

USS Hornet (CV-8). *Courtesy Pete Comer*

Robert "Bobby" Walker. *Courtesy Bobby Walker*

Jonathan Safrit, VMI student, places a wreath at the Tomb of the Unknown Soldier in honor of Combat Airmen/Joshua's Troops. *Courtesy Pete Comer*

Harvey Alexander. *Courtesy Harvey Alexander*

Colonel Phil Newman. *Courtesy Phil Newman*

Frank Lauten. *Courtesy Frank Lauten*

Japanese POWs in Okinawa. *Courtesy Frank Lauten*

Colonel J. Shelton Scales. *Courtesy Shelton Scales*

Colonel John Paul McNeil. *Courtesy John Paul McNeil*

James "Radio" Lawson. *Courtesy Sarah Lawson*

Ken Crowder. *Courtesy Ken Crowder*

Rudolph Joyce. *Courtesy Rudolph Joyce*

Preston Bolick. *Courtesy Preston Bolick*

Thomas McCollum. *Courtesy Thomas McCollum*

Bob Porter, Majuro Island (Marshall Islands). *Courtesy Bob Porter*

Fred Shelton. *Courtesy Fred Shelton*

Howard Gurley. *Courtesy Pat Ransone*

Crew of B-29, Double Trouble. Elmer Jones is 4th from left, 2nd row, standing. *Courtesy Ernest Jones*

Orville Mabe, T-Bone Ridge, Korea. *Courtesy Orville Mabe*

Alexander Worth (left) and Colonel Wm. O. Darby. *Courtesy Alex Worth*

John Bigelow. *Courtesy John Bigelow*

Bill Freeman. *Courtesy Bill Freeman*

John Paul McNeil

When I left there [Korea], I vowed I would never be cold again.

In late 1942, First Lieutenant John Paul McNeil said goodbye to his bride of twelve months to be swept away by the bloody tide of war in the Pacific. As combat landing embarkation officer, he was responsible for preparing and executing unit movement of troops. This was done in accordance with tactical logistic requirements. He set up and participated in landings on major islands including Saipan in the Mariannas, Leyte and Lingayen in the Philippines, and Okinawa in the Ryukyus.

McNeil was born in Wilkes Barre, Pennsylvania, in 1920, into a world ablaze with radical changes in technology, fashion, and lifestyle—a reaction to the stark rationing and sacrifice surrounding World War I. He attended high school at Kingston High, lettering in both football and wrestling. It was football, however, that earned him a scholarship to the University of Maryland, where he was also undefeated in wrestling. Fifty-eight years later, he was inducted into the university's Athletic Hall of Fame. In a letter dated October 20, 1999, recommending McNeil for that high honor, Lieutenant General Louis Metzger (US Marine Corps, retired) wrote the following: "During my thirty-four years of active duty, I knew of no one that better personified the title *Marine* ... Any honor that will be given to Paul will be well deserved."

While still in college, the student-athlete was introduced to Virginia Ditzel, a beautiful freshman. "I was more than a little interested," he admits. "I asked her out, but she turned me down. I thought I was being scorned. Two weeks later, I received a wonderful surprise when I answered the telephone and heard Virginia's voice on the other end: 'Paul, I would like you to be my escort to the sorority spring formal.'" After that first date, both knew they would spend their lives together, sparking a courtship that continued through sixty-two years of marriage.

McNeil made a second important decision during his years in Maryland; he joined the Army ROTC. When he graduated in 1941, he was commissioned second lieutenant. One month later, he decided he would rather be a leatherneck. It took an additional month for him to obtain the same commission in the Marines. He went to Quantico, Virginia, for officer training; then, although he preferred to go overseas, he was held at Quantico to instruct other officer candidates. Advised he would remain stateside for at least a year, he and Virginia married. He deployed twelve months later and was away two and a half years. Virginia wrote him every day.

Strange things happen in war zones. While on an island south of Leyte, where McNeil was on loan to the Army, his unit came under air-raid alert. He dove for a nearby foxhole, colliding in his haste with another GI seeking the same shelter. As the two settled into the relative safety of their hole, they looked up at each other and recognized they were first cousins.

McNeil was in Okinawa when the Japanese, who had vowed to "fight to the last man," surrendered—the result of atomic bomb attacks on Hiroshima and Nagasaki. The lieutenant was chosen to sail by Navy vessel to Yokohama and deliver a sealed message, the contents of which were unknown to him. He assumed they had something to do with the rules of surrender. He and his companion, Sergeant Hale, were the first Americans to enter the port city after hostilities ceased. The port was eerily vacant, with abandoned warehouses stretching along each side. Knowing there could be enemy soldiers—unwilling to accept defeat—skulking in the shadows, he ordered Sergeant Hale to walk behind him *backward*, creating a situation wherein each man covered the other's back.

Thankfully, the duo arrived at their destination unharmed. They were alerted to the gravity with which the Imperial Army viewed the exchange when the Japanese officer—impeccably attired in dress uniform, sword swinging impressively by his side—came to greet them. The Americans, anticipating an informal handoff of papers, wore their traveling clothes: dirty, worn fatigues.

Prior to entering the Korean Conflict in early 1952, McNeil served two months with occupation forces in Japan, followed by a shorter tenure in China. He was combat battalion executive officer in charge of 1,150 men who were, for nine months, the first line of resistance facing North Korean and Chinese forces. "We fought at night," he explains. "The enemy would not come out during the day, due to American air superiority.

"Our orders were to drop back to our line as soon as we made contact. But our opponents soon figured out what we were doing, so we had to hold our position; as soon as we started to move back, our casualties rose. For seventy-two days, the temperature never rose above zero; after dark, it fell to twenty below. It was miserable. When I left there, I vowed I would never be cold again." McNeil was awarded the Bronze Star with Combat V for his service in Korea.

After Korea, McNeil was sent to Yale University in New Haven, Connecticut, to work in the Naval ROTC program. Later, he served at Marine Corps Headquarters in Arlington, Virginia. The McNeil family, including sons J. Paul and Mark, born in 1947 and 1954, respectively, lived in Camp Lejeune for a while before the battle-tested Marine was ordered back to Japan. This time, he was allowed to take his family. "Virginia loved it," he declares. "After two months, she told me that 'all was forgiven'— all the long separations and sleepless nights." One of McNeil's favorite memories is of climbing Mount Fuji with his sons. Reaching the summit just as dawn broke, seven-year-old Mark looked down on the clouds and asked, "What's all that white stuff?"

In 1962, while his family remained in Mount Vernon, McNeil traveled to Laos, Cambodia, Thailand, and Vietnam with Marine Task Force 79 to perform reconnaissance and make preparation for US entry into the war. He served as liaison between American forces and those of his host countries. Once, he came under fire while making aerial surveillance by helicopter; it came so close that the guard dog sitting at his side was killed.

When the veteran of three wars returned to the states, he was made full colonel and transferred to Marine Corps Headquarters in Washington, DC, assigned to research and development. He served on a committee with members of the Department of Defense and the Department of the Navy to determine the needs of troops in the field and respond accordingly.

In 1969, as the Vietnam War continued to rage, Colonel McNeil was asked to return to battle one last time to command a combat regiment. With that achievement on his record, his chances for receiving a highly competitive promotion to general would be greatly enhanced. He talked it over with Virginia, who replied, "I've followed you everywhere for twenty-seven years; I don't want to lose you now." McNeil retired. In addition to the Korean decoration, he was honored with the Marine Headquarters Legion of Merit and at least twenty-five medals, ribbons, and military awards.

Remembering his vow to "never be cold again," the colonel moved his family to Florida the day after his official retirement. He lost his beloved Virginia in 2003, but continues to live in the Sunshine State with son Mark. His older son, J. Paul, lives in Greensboro, and Paul's daughter, McNeil's only grandchild, resides in nearby High Point.

Phil Newman

You were up there, six hundred miles into German territory, and they could get you anytime they wanted.

Retired Air Force Colonel Phil Newman is a man with a mission: he wants to educate the present generation of Americans on the sacrifices that were made to assure the freedoms we often take for granted. To that end, he has worked tirelessly since 1995, when he helped organize Combat Airmen of World War II, a Rockingham County–based veterans' organization. The group went into local and surrounding schools and colleges to talk about World War II and display wartime memorabilia. Ken Samuelson, a volunteer interviewer, audiotaped members' personal experiences, attached the tapes to copies of their war records, and placed them in the Department of Archives in Raleigh, where they remain on permanent display.

Upon graduating high school in Greensboro, Newman moved to Paterson, New Jersey, where he worked for a machine company that manufactured products for the Navy. He admits that he was impressed with the uniformed personnel with whom he came in contact. "Also, my interest in flying was kindled as I watched huge airplanes streak across the New York skyline. Consequently, in June, 1942, I traveled to Newark and enlisted in the United States Army Air Corps as an aviation cadet."

After a year of intense mind and body conditioning, beginning with basic training in Atlantic City, New Jersey, and progressing through a series of increasingly specialized instruction at a number of other schools and bases, Newman graduated as a flight officer and received his wings at Stuttgart, Arkansas. "I had previously requested assignment to the B-17, a four-engine bomber. However, when I reported to Tyndall Field in Florida as ordered, I was led to a B-24 four-engine plane. I had heard that this particular airplane was notorious for developing gasoline leaks, blowing up, and presenting a myriad of serious problems during flight. Yet here I was, being prepared for an orientation flight. Suddenly, a jeep came speeding across the field. A colonel stepped out and yelled, 'Newman, you're at the wrong field! You're supposed to be on the other side of this place, at the B-17s.' Whew. What a relief."

A B-17 pilot with a crew of ten, the young officer was assigned to the 99th Bomb Group and the 347th Bomb Squadron. His permanent base was Foggia, Italy. From there, he flew missions to Vienna, Prague, Berlin, Innsbruck, and cities of northern Italy. "We bombed targets such as bridges, ammunition factories, fighter factories, oil refineries, and rail yards," he recalls.

Newman explodes the myth that bomber pilots live a life of revelry and glamour. He says that every day he flew a mission was a bad day—sometimes that was four or five days in a row, sometimes three. He explains, "When a pilot saw his name on the battle order for the following day, he went to his cot and wrote a letter home. He had orders to place all of his belongings—along with the letter—on the end of his cot before leaving the next morning. One of the pilots' duties when not flying was to go through the possessions of airmen who did not return and remove anything that would cause unnecessary pain to the family." Newman went to bed about 8:00 p.m. on the eve of a flight.

The day of a mission began at 2:00 a.m. with a cold shave; the shave was essential to allow the oxygen mask to fit properly. Newman and the other pilots had breakfast, composed of powdered eggs, fried Spam, marmalade, coffee, dried milk, and sometimes cereal. Afterward, they attended a fifteen- to twenty-minute pilot briefing, during which time a large map outlining their target for the day was displayed. At that point, anyone who felt the need could speak with a chaplain. Then, dressed in underwear and flying suits, they climbed aboard a truck, rode by to pick up their parachutes, which were housed at a separate location on base, and advanced to the flight line.

"I remember once when we also picked up a package of 'Red Seal' money—four hundred and twenty dollars for each crew member. This was to be used to buy our way to safety if we were shot down. Toward the end of the war, however, this practice was abandoned; instead, we carried documents in our uniform pockets, allowing us to ask for help. If aid was given, we could sign a receipt, which would be honored by the United States government."

By the time the pilots arrived at their planes, the ground crew would have already loaded the twelve five-hundred-pound bombs usually carried by each. "One day, I came out to the plane and saw them cranking something up in the bomb bay doors after they had loaded the bombs. 'What is that?' I asked. It turns out that the ground crew had sealed and loaded a *field toilet*. Each one of them had written a message to Hitler on it." The flight crew always went through a final checklist to make sure everything was in proper working order. A flare would be shot from the tower, indicating that it was time to start the engines and get in a line—sometimes half a mile long. The planes took off one right after the other, flying in tight formation, almost wing tip to wing tip, to deter attack by the Germans.

As soon as they reached enemy territory, somewhere around lunchtime, they began to see flak, especially in the large towns like Vienna and Prague. The bomb run was approximately fifteen miles long and took anywhere from eight to ten minutes. Newman shakes his head as he says, "I don't know how many antiaircraft guns were shooting at one time, but there must have been thousands of them because they didn't quit. How they missed some of those planes, I'll never know. Some of them got direct hits and blew up. Some got their engines shot off. It was a slaughter, really. The attrition rate was often as high as 20 percent."

Immediately after their bombs were dropped, the pilots headed for home. If possible, they held formation all the way because German fighters were looking for stragglers and crippled planes. According to

Newman, "You were up there, six hundred miles into German territory, and they could get you anytime they wanted; but along about that time, the German oil supply had been depleted to the point that they could not afford to defend anything but Berlin and a couple of the larger cities."

In March 1945, while returning from a mission to Vienna, Newman lost an engine and fell dangerously behind his formation. "A P-51 pulled up on my right wing—wheels and flaps lowered in an effort to slow the airplane enough to fly with my B-17. The pilot opened his canopy and pulled his oxygen mask down; I could see that he was a Tuskegee Airman." Newman pauses to reflect and smiles. "I learned that Tuskegee Airman had followed me for about five hundred miles, protecting me from German attack."

The pilots usually arrived back at home base—anywhere from 3:00 p.m. to 4:00 p.m.—exhausted. They would have been in the air from eight to twelve hours with no food, no bathing facility, and no bathroom. They routinely exited their planes leaving everything behind except parachutes, which they were required to turn in. While ground crews worked to get planes ready for the next day's flights, flight crews attended debriefing, which usually lasted thirty minutes or so. They were then free to get something to eat—more Spam and GI bread. At 6:00 p.m., they went to headquarters to check the battle order. If they were flying the following morning, they made the necessary preparations and turned in early.

Germany surrendered on May 7, 1945; May 8 was declared Victory in Europe (VE) Day. Newman had flown fifty combat missions. After the war ended, he flew fifteen additional missions, going into at least eight different countries to search for prisoners of war and concentration camps. "If the Russians found Allied POWs before we did," he points out, "they would carry them to Russia and put them in labor camps."

After his official release from military service, Newman and his wife, Blanche Triska Newman, moved to Greensboro, where he eventually started his own business in the communications industry. The pair was blessed with two children, Charles and Phyllis. Blanche passed away in

2003, after fifty-nine years of marriage. In 2007, Charles lost his twenty-five-year battle with multiple sclerosis.

The retired pilot eventually moved to Gainesville, Florida, where he resides with his current wife, Aurelia Dunston Wallace. He continues to pursue his passion through participation in various veterans' organizations: the Decrepit Birdmen of World War II is made up of forty-five pilots and crew members. They speak at approximately eight schools or universities each month and appear in air shows in Ocala and Keystone Heights, where they talk about the warbirds (B-17s, B-24s and B-25s), which are on display.

Newman is also an active member of the Military Support Group of Alachua County, an organization which meets twice each month and prepares up to 120 packages to be mailed to troops overseas. Additionally, he belongs to the Fifteenth Air Force Association, the Experimental Aircraft Association, the Antique Airways Association, the Veterans of Foreign Wars, the American Legion, the Disabled American Veterans, the Marine Corps League, the Alachua County Veterans Advisory Board, and the Pilot Class 1944 Association.

Newman's most recent project, Home Front, involves enlisting wives of World War II veterans to share with audiences how they dealt with rationing, shortages, entering the work force, and generally taking care of home and family while their husbands were away.

Bob Porter

I was tapped to go to the Marshall Islands as part of Task Force 132, charged with detonating the first hydrogen bomb.

66 "I don't consider myself a hero by any stretch of the imagination," begins Bob Porter. "I spent twenty-eight years in the Air Force and never fired a shot at anybody, and I don't know that anybody ever fired a shot at me." Porter goes on to admit that he initially set out to dodge the draft. "It was 1949; I was in my second year of college, and the draft was closing in. I tried to join the Navy like my older brother, but apparently the Navy recruiter had met his quota, because he referred me to the Air Force." And so it was that in September 1950, Robert Porter of Wythe County, Virginia, second eldest of seven siblings, turned his eyes toward "the wild blue yonder."

Porter traveled to Wichita Falls, Texas, for basic training, an endeavor he calls "a breeze for a country boy accustomed to hard work." He went from there to technical school in Mississippi, to learn to be a radio operator. Asked what that position entailed, he explains, "While on a mission, radio operators relayed position reports hourly—indicating the aircraft's longitude and latitude. Additionally, they transmitted 'operation normal' reports every half hour, advising the ground crew that they were still in the air. If an hour passed with no word from an airplane, a search-by-radio was instigated. If two hours passed, search planes were launched."

Porter's first assignment was flying B-29s at Barksdale Air Force Base in Louisiana. "I will never get over the shock of walking out on the flight line and seeing guns sticking out of the airplanes." I thought, "What have

I gotten myself into?" After training on the B-29s for over a year, Porter assumed he would be sent to Korea, like the other radio operators in his class. But instead, he was tapped to go to the Marshall Islands as part of Task Force 132, charged with detonating the first hydrogen bomb.

"That was the most important thing I did in my career," he says. "I was at about three thousand feet, ninety miles east of ground zero when the bomb went off. I listened to the countdown over the radio: 'five, four, three, two—*turn your eyes away*!' I turned away, and in my position in the airplane, I was in the dark. When it detonated, it lit up my dark corner from ninety miles away, so I *knew* it was powerful. We had calculated it would take us ten minutes to receive the shockwave. Almost exactly ten minutes later, we felt the plane shake."

After that, Task Force 132 was supposed to return to the states but instead remained with the Army on Enewetak, a two- by three-quarter-mile island, for the next year—their status changing from temporary duty to permanent change of station. Later, Porter would also live for a time with the Navy on Kwajalein, part of the Pacific missile test range used for military purposes by the Americans after they captured it from the Japanese in 1944.

Porter's next assignment was Patrick Air Force Base in Florida, home of the Atlantic Missile Test Range. He routinely carried supplies and mail to tracking stations up and down the Bahamas. But one of his major responsibilities was to fly around the Cape Canaveral launch area in a B-17 and clear the area of shrimp boats that had ignored previous warnings to stay away. "We would pass over them and lead them out of danger," he remembers. "Sometimes they would not respond, and we would get down close enough to rock their boat. If a missile had to be aborted right after liftoff, anyone within a ten-mile radius would be in danger."

The airman completed his first four-year hitch in September 1954; in October, he married Barbara Priddy of Mayodan. He purchased a brand new, baby blue 1954 Bel Air Chevrolet, and he and Barbara toured the New England states for their honeymoon. Unable to find work that appealed to him, and "after much soul searching and prayer," he reenlisted in the Air Force on December 1, 1954. "I didn't discuss it with Barbara," he confesses, "but being part gypsy, she was thrilled." The couple returned to Florida and rented a one-bedroom apartment in which a kerosene heater in the bathroom provided their only source of hot water. Barbara found a clerical job, and they settled in. Six months later, they received notice that the groom was being deployed.

Given a choice of two assignments—Hickam Field in Hawaii or Kwajalein Air Base in the Marshall Islands—Porter responded quickly, "No competition; I'll take Hawaii." Off-base housing was arranged near Hickam, and the couple drove to San Francisco, boarded a ship, and sailed to beautiful Honolulu, Hawaii. Unfortunately, their treasured Bel Air had to be shipped by slow boat, so the resourceful pair purchased a Cushman Scooter to transport themselves around the island while they waited. Finally, word arrived that they could go to the dock and claim their automobile. "Our beautiful Chevrolet looked like it had been through multiple tornados," laments Porter, who set to work immediately, restoring his prize to its former luster. They still had the car when they left the island four years later.

"We enjoyed our stay at Hickam Air Base," recalls Porter. "Separation was the only drawback. Our unit flew all over the South Pacific: Guam, the Philippines, Okinawa, Vietnam, Japan. If we flew west, we would be gone anywhere from one to three weeks. Our wives never knew when to expect us, but the base would call our homes when we were on our last leg of flight—primarily to allow any *unauthorized* males who might be visiting to clear out before husbands arrived." Some days, Porter did not have to report to base; he called in twice daily to receive instructions.

Midway through his Hawaiian tour, radio equipment became so sophisticated that operators were no longer needed to send coded messages; pilots could call in their own reports. A request was forwarded to Headquarters Air Force, asking that radio operators be allowed to cross-train for Military Air Transport Service (MATS). Loadmasters were needed to get cargo on and off aircraft, care for the cargo during flight, load paratroopers, and open doors for the paratroopers to jump. They would also be in charge of dropping heavy equipment, such as jeeps, tanks, or trucks. "In the meantime, the first class of trainees was sent ahead before permission came. I was in that class," proclaims Porter appreciatively.

After six weeks of training in Palm Beach, Florida, Porter returned to Hawaii, where he assumed the role of loadmaster, transferring to C-124 cargo planes. But the Air Force turned down the unit's request to allow radio operators to retrain for MATS, reasoning that they were needed in other locations. "I was really fortunate," Porter points out. "All the other places that needed radio operators, you didn't want to go—Thule Air Base in Greenland."

From Hawaii, the Porters returned to Barksdale Air Force Base. He describes his job there as "moving nuclear weapons around: they had to be carried to the factory for upgrading, overhauling, or general maintenance. We would go around to all the Strategic Air Command [SAC] bases, pick them up, take them to be repaired, and return them to base." The Porters understood that they would remain in Louisiana for a long period of time, so they purchased a home. Eighteen months later, they were transferred to Evreux Air Base in France, where the family— which now included two sons—once again lived on the local economy, in a lovely new apartment.

Porter shares that one of the high points of his French tour came when John Glenn made his first orbit around the earth: "We had a helicopter waiting in Nairobi, Kenya. If he had to go down in the Indian Ocean, it was going to be that helicopter's job to pluck him out of the water. Fortunately, he didn't go down, so we came on back." Other fond memories include traveling "all over Europe, Africa, India, and Asia."

Frank Leonard, a young airman, and his new wife were friends of the Porters. Mrs. Leonard was staying with them while her husband was on a mission to Nairobi. Porter received word that Leonard's plane had gone down. He immediately telephoned the base: "Frank Leonard's wife is staying at my house," he reported. They thanked him and hung up.

A few minutes later, the phone rang, and a voice on the other end asked, "Where is your house?"

Porter raced home to let Barbara know—privately—that a chaplain and flight surgeon were on their way to advise their houseguest that her husband had been killed. Soon, a military vehicle pulled up. Porter pauses and shakes his head, "It took that chaplain *forever* to get the words out."

Leonard's squadron leader asked Porter to escort the widow back to the states. He accompanied her to New Jersey, where her husband's family lived. The senior Leonard wanted to know if his son had been in any way responsible for what had happened. "I assured him that he was *not*, and I believe that gave him some peace," opines Porter, who left satisfied that he had completed his mission successfully.

Before American personnel were scheduled to leave France, word arrived that the French government wanted them out. The entire wing— three squadrons of sixteen planes each—rotated back to Lockbourne Air Force Base in Columbus, Ohio. "We loved Ohio," stresses Porter, who was promoted to senior master sergeant while there. "We stayed eight years. It was the only place where Barbara cried when we left. We made some dear friends at the church there; we still get Christmas cards from some of them."

From Ohio, Porter was transferred to Pope Air Force Base, where the youngest of his three sons was born. He requested that site because of its close proximity to the Mayodan property he had purchased in 1964. He could go there on weekends and work on his twenty-four-acre plat of land. Porter retired on December 31, 1979. By the time that date rolled around, he had built a garage suitable for storing his household goods and purchased a mobile home in which to live while he worked on his house—completed five years later. The industrious couple did all the labor themselves, except for brickwork in the chimney and foundation. "When we came up on something we didn't know how to do, we stopped working and took a class," acknowledges Porter.

Pressed for reflections on his career in military service, Porter responds thoughtfully, "I don't believe it is the intention of the Air Force that anyone should ever get a raw deal. I would recommend it to anybody who is so inclined."

Hassel Priddy

A huge wave washed one sailor overboard,
and another swept him back on deck.

Hassel Priddy sits across the table from me in his comfortable Mayodan home, doing his best to ignore the miniature tape recorder hovering conspicuously to his left. "I graduated high school May 5, 1943, and was inducted in the Army the following July 14. I took basic training at Camp Wallace in Galveston, Texas, the hottest place I had ever been. Because I could type, I was assigned to clerical school and proclaimed a typist. The truth is, I always *hated* typing. I flew to England May 13, 1944, where we prepared for the D-day landing on Normandy."

My host takes a deep breath, glances at the tape recorder and frowns, and then launches into an explanation of ADSEC, to which he was assigned: "It stands for Advanced Section Transportation Corps. We followed the First, Third, and Ninth Armies through France, Holland, Belgium, Luxembourg, and into Germany, making sure they had all the supplies they needed to push the Germans back."

Before ADSEC, invading US armies were responsible for requisition and maintenance of their own supplies. But with the March 1944 formation of this unique advance team, that burden was gradually lifted from the shoulders of the fighting men. The new company—to which service units stationed throughout the United Kingdom were reassigned—included both a Signal Corps and a Corps of Engineers.

Priddy's group arrived in Normandy mid-July, *after* the June 6 invasion. They lived in pup tents, ate K-rations, dug slit trenches, and dodged artillery and flak from strafing German aircraft. Theirs was the first transportation company to follow immediately on the heels of advancing armies. Priddy's job was to take telephone calls from supply units on the beaches and apprise the armies—through coded messages—of which supplies were forthcoming. American forces pushed the Germans back from Cherbourg and Carentan, with divisions of ADSEC enabling their advance by rebuilding docks, repairing locomotives, and clearing wreckage.

On July 25, the skies over Saint-Lô thundered as wave after wave of American bombers dropped their deadly missiles, reducing the area to shambles. "I watched it all. It was devastating," recalls Priddy. The German army, pursued vigorously by US forces, retreated to LeMans and then to Entampes, where weary GIs relaxed and enjoyed a musical visit from Dinah Shore, Bing Crosby, and Fred Astaire. The respite was brief, however, because America was on the move, and ADSEC was part of the action. It was not long before news of the liberation of Paris rocked the world.

The Allies pushed the Germans as far as Reims, where opposing armies fought violently for forty-seven days. Afterward, the victorious Allies chased Hitler's fleeing residue of troops across the border into Belgium, capturing the city of Lemur on October 25. It was about this time that Priddy was sent to Maastricht, Holland, for a brief tenure. While there, he was relieved of clerical duties, including the dreaded typing, so that he could drive a jeep.

What he enjoyed least while in the Netherlands was the B-2 unmanned bombers. "They sounded like little cub planes," he explains. "If you could hear them coming, you knew you were alright; but when they cut off, you knew they were coming down—you just didn't know where. Once while I was sitting on the side of the bunk, I heard them coming. Some of the guys headed for the air-raid shelter a few miles away, but I just sat there—frozen. That was probably the closest I ever came to being hit."

By December 16, 1944, Priddy had rejoined his outfit and was in Verdun, France, headed for Namur, Belgium. The German Army launched a desperate counteroffensive through the Ardennes toward the Meuse River, targeting ADSEC's large supply dump. American units were subjected to bombing, strafing, tanks, small artillery fire, and mine attacks. The fierce fighting that ensued became known as the Battle of the Bulge, a reference to the large bulge created in the Allied lines during the initial attack. By the following January, despite sustaining some seventy-five thousand casualties, America had reclaimed all territory lost to the Nazis.

ADSEC built a pontoon bridge across the Rhine, and the Germans were shoved back across their own border, forcing them to confront the ravages of war in their homeland. While in Bonn, Priddy and his friends spent a couple of weeks in an abandoned house: "We ate food from the basement and kitchen and dug potatoes in the garden," he tells me, smiling at the pleasant memory. "That was nice." The Allies advanced as far as Fulda, situated in the heart of Germany. At that point, the Third Reich had nowhere to run.

Priddy was in England on May 8, 1945, when the war in Europe ended. He returned to Paris to serve until he had accumulated enough points to come home. He kept busy waterproofing equipment for shipment to the states. Little did he know that one of his scariest moments lay just ahead.

He was sailing back to America aboard the USS *George Washington* on December 12 when the sea turned deadly. For nine days, the ship rode the waves, the crew battling seventy mile-per-hour winds. The rudder snapped under the pressure, and brave Seabees suffered broken arms and legs attempting to make repairs. "A huge wave washed one sailor overboard; another swept him back on deck. I didn't think we would make it," admits Priddy.

Priddy made his postwar home in Mayodan but for a while commuted to nearby Guilford County to work with the Greensboro-based Military Training Camp and Overseas Replacement Depot (ORD). He later worked with Gama Hosiery and Gem Dandy Inc. of Madison. On November 6, 1947, he married Doris Richardson, and in 1952, the couple built a house on Peach Orchard Road. At about the same time, they planted a hundred peach trees—a modest beginning for what has become Priddy's Peach Orchard, which has provided the surrounding area with the succulent fruit for over fifty years. The Priddys have one son, three grandchildren, and two great-grandchildren.

J. Shelton Scales

I knew I was going to die—no ifs, ands, maybes, buts, or whatevers.

D-day on Iwo Jima turned out to be the bloodiest battle in the history of the Marine Corps: of the approximately 22,000 Japanese participating in the fighting, roughly 21,000 were killed, and 6,821 Americans lost their lives. Predicted to last about ten days, the siege went on for thirty-six, thanks to the tenacity of the experienced Japanese troops defending the island. In the end, America prevailed, marking the first capture of Japanese home territory of the war.

Just five years prior to taking part in the historic landing, J. Shelton Scales was claiming his degree from the University of North Carolina–Chapel Hill. Shortly after returning to his home in Stoneville, he received a letter from the dean of the university, explaining that he had been asked by the commandant of the Marine Corps to recommend approximately 5 percent of the graduating class for Marine officer training. Scales was being asked if he would like to participate. At first, he was not interested, but the more he thought about it, the more sense it made. The war in Europe had been escalating since its inception in September 1939. He was healthy and single, and registration for the draft would begin in October. He likely would have been one of the first drafted, and he felt an aversion to being "pushed in." Finally, he sought advice from Clarence Stone—then state representative, later state senator—who advised him to "go ahead and sign up; it would be good to get a commission." He went to Raleigh the next day and enlisted.

Scales reported to the Marine Corps base in Quantico, Virginia, on November 1, 1940, for thirteen weeks of basic training. In February, he was commissioned second lieutenant and given three months of additional instruction on leading a platoon, reading a map, conducting communications, and understanding the Army manual of organized warfare; for example, if captured, give only your name, rank, and serial number. Since America had not yet entered the war—it was now May 1941— Scales was sent back to the company in which he had served as private first class. Ironically, the same noncommissioned officers who had once given him a hard time found themselves saluting him instead. Lieutenant Scales remained there as an instructor in Officer Candidate School until July 1943.

Sandwiched between the preparatory years of higher learning and military training and the savage years of war, Scales experienced the happiest period of his young life. While in college, he had met a beautiful undergraduate named Stacey Crockett and was immediately smitten. He recalls declaring, "I am going to marry this gal if she will have me." She would. They were married New Year's Day, 1942. The couple *was* to be married in June 1942, but the Japanese bombed Pearl Harbor on December 7, 1941. The wedding was moved up because there was uncertainty as to where the bridegroom would be on the later date. They were married in the bride's home church in Bluefield, Virginia.

On August 7, 1942, three things happened that dramatically altered Scales's circumstances: first, he was promoted to captain; next, he was given a job he considers to be the best in the Marine Corps, commanding a company of officer candidates; and finally, the Marines landed on Guadalcanal. The captain was ordered to Camp Pendleton, California, to join the developing Fourth Marine Division. He and a buddy traveled cross-country in a 1937 Plymouth, arriving in eight days despite slick tires and rationed gas. Scales, given command of Alpha Company, First Battalion, Twenty-Third Marines, studied weaponry and military tactics and practiced amphibious landings off San Clemente Island.

On January 13, 1944, Scales and his comrades set out from San Diego—combat loaded—for the Marshall Islands. They landed in the northern end of Kwajalein on February 1, 1944, capturing the small island, along with its valuable airfield, in a single day. The Marines later described this battle as a "cake walk" compared to what they encountered in future landings. Mission accomplished, the men returned to their base camp in Maui, Hawaii, where the twenty-thousand-man division continued training. Scales was promoted to major in April.

After capturing the Solomon, Gilbert, and Marshall Islands, the Allies were ready to tackle the main Japanese defense line, which included the Mariana Islands. The Marianas were deemed important because of the appearance of the new B-29 long-range bomber, which boasted a range of 3,500 miles. From the Marianas, Tokyo fell well within that range.

Eight thousand Marines, including Scales, landed on the coast of Saipan on June 15, 1944. By nightfall, despite heavy losses, they had secured a beachhead about six miles wide and one-half mile deep. The Japanese troops were woefully outnumbered but determined to fight to the last man. During the day, they hid in the numerous caves that dotted the landscape; at night, they counterattacked. The Americans learned to clear the caves with the aid of flamethrowers. By July 9, Saipan was officially secured. Shamed, Lieutenant General Yoshitsugu Saito, commander of the Forty-Third Division of the Imperial Japanese Army, committed suicide inside a cave.

American troops sought unsuccessfully to persuade Japanese civilians to surrender, but they had been convinced that American and British forces were barbarians who treated prisoners of war inhumanely. Hundreds of them chose instead to take their own lives, many by jumping from cliffs. When it was all over, twenty-two thousand Japanese civilians were dead, as were about thirty thousand Japanese warriors. The victory cost Americans more than had any Pacific War battle to date: of the seventy-one thousand who landed, more than fourteen thousand were killed, wounded, or missing.

After Saipan, Scales and his companions were given one week to make plans before landing on Tinian, an island three miles south of Saipan. In what has been called "the perfect amphibious operation," the island was taken in eight to nine days. Major Scales and his battalion captured part of the airfield from which the crew of the *Enola Gay* took off on August 6, 1945—headed for Hiroshima, Japan, to drop the first atomic bomb ever used in war.

Scales, executive officer of the First Battalion, second in command, came back from the Marianas in late August 1944. On October 2, he was notified that the regimental commanding officer wanted to see him in his office right away. *What have I done or failed to do?* wondered Scales as he was being escorted to the meeting, during which he stood at attention the entire time.

The colonel shifted the ever-present cigar in his mouth and barked, "Scales, I want you to go down and take charge of that Third Battalion and shape 'em up."

Scales, shocked into silence, considered saying, "Thank you, Colonel, but I believe I'll pass." Knowing, however, that refusal was not an option, he called the sergeant major of the Third Battalion and asked to speak to all the officers and noncoms who would be under his command—about 1,500. He introduced himself and told them how he planned to operate and what he would expect of them. They spent some time getting accustomed to the feel and routine of the new situation, and then on New Year's Eve, they loaded into a new troop ship and sailed for Pearl Harbor. After the ship's crew had an opportunity to practice checking and lowering boats, they headed toward Saipan, their objective being about seven hundred miles north of there—a Japanese home island called Iwo Jima.

US Marines landed on heavily fortified Iwo Jima on February 19, 1945. The First and Second Battalions were the first to go ashore, while the Third Battalion—commanded by Scales—waited expectantly on the line of departure for orders to enter the fray. They came about one o'clock in the afternoon. The colonel's instructions were simple: "Go in, pass through the First Battalion, and continue the attack." Scales notified his people, and they began to move forward; he followed in the sixth wave.

Japanese soldiers positioned atop Mount Suribachi, a 556-foot extinct volcano, saw them coming. They rained artillery and mortar fire up and down the crawling beach, slaughtering 2,400 men in one day. Scales, no stranger to frontline combat, could find only one word to describe what he witnessed all about him—*carnage*.

The Americans desperately needed Iwo Jima to use as an emergency landing strip for damaged B-29s returning from Japan. The limping superfortresses, unable to make it all the way back to Saipan, were being forced to ditch in the Pacific Ocean, resulting in serious loss of planes and personnel. Before their objective could be achieved, however, they would have to take possession of Suribachi, an obstruction that hovered over the five-mile-long, two-and-a-half-mile-wide, eight-mile-square island like a giant eye in the sky. The Fifth Marine Division, one of two divisions to land on the island, was charged with securing the mountain, a task requiring four days of intense fighting.

Scales, with the Fourth Division, was about two miles north at that time. Suddenly, one of his men called out, "What is that on Suribachi?" Scales strained to see. It looked like a flag, but was it American or Japanese? He reached for his binoculars. Focusing in, he was able to make out the Stars and Stripes waving triumphantly in the breeze. Jubilation erupted: grateful men jumped up and down, fired their weapons, hugged, shouted, and gave thanks.

"It was the *second* most beautiful sight I had ever seen," remembers Scales, "the *first* being, of course, my bride on our wedding day."

After Scales returned to his home base in Hawaii, he and eighteen to twenty other officers were summoned to the regimental commander's residence. On arrival, they encountered an armed guard at the door, a precaution they considered unusual since they were thousands of miles away from a combat zone. They were directed to a table overlaid with a sheet. "Gentlemen," announced the commander as he removed the cover, "here is your next objective—Wake Island." America was getting ready to invade the Japanese home islands, and they would need this northern Pacific island to use as an airfield for refueling planes.

Scales's division started training immediately for the landing, set for October 1, 1945. In the meantime, they began to hear rumors of a Japanese city being hit with a bomb equal to twenty thousand tons of TNT. The Marines laughed at the idea, certain that there could be "no such animal." A few nights later, Scales overheard a conversation involving the regimental adjutant, indicating that the war was over. He and others broke out the champagne and began to celebrate. The party lasted long into the night; but alas, the next morning, they learned that it had been a false alarm. Three days later, while Scales and his men were in the field training, the Japanese surrendered. A truck convoy was dispatched to bring them back to base, where the entire regiment took part in a memorial service.

How had Scales regarded the prospect of taking part in the Wake Island landing— his *fifth*? "I had used up a whole lot of luck," he assures me. "On those other four, I had never had the conviction that I was going to be killed. I might get wounded, but nothing too bad, just enough maybe to get me back to the states. On this one, I *knew* I was going to die—no ifs, ands, maybes, buts, or whatevers. It preyed on me; I damn near became an alcoholic. For a while, I would get about sloshed every night. When it was officially over, I could relate to what a person on death row feels when he is pardoned."

Scales returned to home and Stacey in 1945, having devoted five long, hard years to the defense of his country. In May 1946, he joined Burch Hodges-Stone, Inc., an independent insurance agency in Martinsville, Virginia. He was part of the company for thirty-six years, the last nine of which he served as president. He was married two months shy of sixty-five years. Even now, when he speaks of his wife, who passed away on November 6, 2006, his voice becomes soft, reverent. Stacey Scales is survived not only by her husband, but also by four children, eight grandchildren, and five great-grandchildren.

In 1951, Scales, a Marine Corps reservist, was promoted to lieutenant colonel. He had spent ten months performing the duties of that office—commanding a battalion. Unexpectedly, in 1957, he was again promoted, this time to colonel. Colonel Scales admits, "I have always been less than enthusiastic about the last promotion, because so many colonels spent twenty-five or thirty years in the Marine Corps commanding regiments. But if they want to give it to me, I'll take it."

As of 2011, Colonel J. Shelton Scales is one of three surviving battalion commanders from Iwo Jima.

Fred Shelton

If it had not been for the Lord, none of us would have made it.

ading in rice paddies up to his neck, with no idea where he was, in darkness as thick as the stalks through which he slogged, Fred Shelton wondered, "Lord, why have you put me in this position?" The twenty-three-year-old Mayodan man had not chosen to go to Vietnam. He had been married three years and held a good position with Fieldcrest Industries. Nevertheless, when his draft notice arrived, he answered the call. He kissed his young wife, Sarah, goodbye and boarded the bus for Fort Bragg. After basic training, he traveled to Fort Knox, Kentucky, for advanced instruction. He was trained in intelligence and made squad leader.

While in Kentucky, he shared his Christian faith with a young man in his outfit who was headed to Vietnam. "Years later," he remembers, " I got a letter from that guy, thanking me and telling me that he had 'seen the light.'"

Before long, Shelton too was shipped overseas—not as intelligence specialist, but as infantryman attached to a search and destroy mission. Based at Placoo, he was struck by the poverty of South Vietnam: houses were little more than cardboard hovels. Since there was no running water, women carried their family's supply from nearby streams. Once, a little girl offered him a cool drink from a gourd. He was grateful but never felt he could completely trust the populace: "They could be your friends in the daytime and turn on you at night."

Village people, called Montagnards, maintained meager existences in grass shacks. As the villagers cultivated gardens to provide food for themselves, North Vietnamese soldiers routinely came and ordered them to package their harvested crops in containers and leave them at specified locations—or face death. "We would go out and seize the enemy caches and return them to the people," reports Shelton, still bristling at the injustice.

One day, a fellow soldier approached Shelton and asked what he needed to do to become a Christian. "I talked with him," recalls the sergeant, "and had him talk with the chaplain. I'm satisfied that he made things right with his Maker. I learned later that he had been killed.

"I saw some action," admits Shelton modestly, "mostly in the jungles of the Central Highlands." GIs there battled not only the North Vietnamese but also the Vietcong. These unconventional warriors excelled in guerrilla tactics, employing various types of homemade booby traps: deadly punji sticks; buckets filled with metal scraps and buried in the ground so as to cut or tear the legs of unwary soldiers; an array of explosive traps fashioned from pilfered grenades. In addition, US forces were bombarded with mortars, small arms fire, bombs, and shrapnel. "When we encountered fire, we returned it. We could hear it coming; mortars made the worst sound.

"Sometimes we would hear that the enemy was hiding in one of the villages. Four or five of us would set up a night patrol to clear them out. We usually had air support: C-130 planes—nicknamed *Puff the Magic Dragons*—armed with twenty-millimeter machine guns, sprayed every two inches of targeted territory. Once we had removed the people and livestock, along with their food, we burned the villages."

Shelton's most frightening experience occurred in the Ia Drang Valley. "We knew the enemy was in the area. The night before we were to go in, a hornet stung me, keeping me out of the hottest part of the battle. Still, I was hit in the knee by shrapnel from a bomb. Bullets and mortars popped overhead nonstop. Eight hundred enemy soldiers were killed in that encounter, as were all except ten of an American sister company. If it had not been for the Lord, none of us would have made it."

Shelton remained in Vietnam one year. He then returned to the United States, completing his tour of duty in California—first at Fort Ord and then at Camp Roberts. He was promoted to sergeant and charged with supervising the maintenance of motor vehicles. "I was witnessing to one of the crew about the Lord," he testifies, "when another young man wanted to talk with me. He didn't want the others to know he was interested, so I went with him to his barracks. He asked me to show him how to roll his socks. I was surprised; a private asking his sergeant to roll socks was unheard of. But I did it. I thought my doing that small service for him might convince him that the Lord is real in my life. I hope so."

The sergeant views his time in the military philosophically: "I gained experience, grew up a lot. I became more aware of the presence of a Supreme Being. If I had just had more faith, I wouldn't have been quite so scared. But if anyone tells you he is *not* scared going into combat, something is wrong with him."

Eventually, Shelton returned to Mayodan and Sarah, but the horrors of jungle warfare continued to invade his dreams. One night, he hit Sarah in the eye while they slept. "It was a hard time," he says. "I don't like to talk about some things."

"I could tell he had been through a bad ordeal," adds Sarah, "because sometimes he wouldn't have anything to say."

His job with Fieldcrest having been filled during his absence, Shelton worked with Burlington Industries twenty years and then with Southern Finishing. He has been a member of Stone-Eden Baptist Church for the past thirty years.

Boyd J. Steele

*If I had to die, I could think of no better way
to go than by fighting for my country.*

66 **I** went down the rope ladder of the landing craft into the waist-deep waters off Omaha Beach. As I waded ashore—gently pushing aside, stepping around and over bodies of men who had fallen the day before—I asked my Lord to be my shepherd and to guide me. If I had to die, I could think of no better way to go than by fighting for my country." Boyd J. Steele relives the anguish of combat as we sit in the living room of his Stoneville home, examining his Purple Heart, along with an array of medals and memorabilia.

March through May 1944 found Steele engaged in rifle training in England. The following month, things began to heat up: On June 3, his squadron was quarantined to the camp area. On June 4, they were issued rifles. On June 5, they boarded a troop ship in the English Channel, bound for France. June 6, at 2:00 a.m., they were given a paper sack and a letter from General Dwight D. Eisenhower, telling them what they could expect. By daybreak, they could hear heavy bombing. *Surely, we won't be in the first assault*, Steele recalls thinking. *We haven't even been issued live ammunition.* On June 7, at first light, they went ashore fully armed. It was D-day plus one.

Steele, assigned to the Fourth Infantry Division, was about a half-mile inland. The Germans were on the run, the Americans advancing day to day. "On June 15, I was walking beside my best friend, Robert South; we had gone through basic training together at Camp Wheeler in Macon, Georgia. We were moving through an apple orchard when we began to take heavy artillery. We ran to a nearby ravine. The shelling lasted from three to five minutes. Suddenly, I missed Robert. He had been hit by a large piece of shrapnel and blown five feet away. When the shelling stopped, I ran to him. He was dead, his body ripped apart by the fragment." Steele leaned over and picked up the projectile—about four inches in length—washed away Robert's blood, and stuck it in his pocket. He keeps it as a remembrance of that day, and of Robert. "Twelve men went into the ravine; seven came out."

After that skirmish, there was moderate infantry advancement with occasional shelling. On July 7, a smoke screen was provided for the bombing of Saint-Lô. "Just as the bombers flew over, the wind shifted, and the smoke drifted back over our troops," recalls Steele. "We were pinned down behind a hedgerow." As Browning Automatic Rifle specialist, he was required to secure ammunition and load clips for the squad. He had three bandoliers of ammunition around his neck when two officers approached the scene.

"They told me to cross the hedgerow and draw enemy fire, while the rest of the squad attacked in the direction of the fire." I hear myself gasp when he tells me this, unable to hide my shock. "It sounded like suicide," he admits. "But I decided I would rather be dead than get a dishonorable discharge. I had gone about ten steps when I could see machine-gun bullets hitting the dirt, racing toward me. The last thing I remember was my rifle being shot away. I ran backward to the hedgerow and dove over it head first, tearing my knee up when I landed. I was hit in the right hip; I couldn't walk. But I could hear the others as they made the attack."

Alone momentarily, Steele crawled into an abandoned German bunker and patched his wounds as best he could. Soon, he heard troops approaching. "I knew from their boots they were American. I called out to them that I was an American soldier and I was hurt. They told me to come out—hands first." He was placed on a stretcher and then into a jeep with another wounded soldier. On the way to a field hospital, medics drew Steele's blood to transfuse their more critical patient, who was accepted at the hospital. Steele, his injuries not considered life-threatening, was carried back to the beach and loaded onto an airplane with twenty or thirty other wounded men for flight to England.

The next morning, a nurse removed Steele's pants and counted *thirteen* bullet holes. Miraculously, he had been hit only once—in the hip. "I believe every one of those bullet holes represents a prayer from somebody," he stresses. He was sent to several hospitals before leaving England. At the last of these, he heard that he had been placed on the ZI list. He was happy to learn that those initials stood for "Zone of the Interior"—America. He boarded ship to sail for the states on Christmas Day, 1944.

"I knew I was home," he jokes, "when I heard a radio blasting the familiar theme song of a favorite children's program: 'Hi-Yo, Silver, Away!'—*The Lone Ranger*." Steele was in hospitals, at home and abroad, for eleven months. Afterward, he was placed on total disability for two years and 10 percent for the remainder of his life.

Asked how, in retrospect, he feels about officers ordering him to present himself as a decoy, Steele replies, without hint of bitterness, "I think they were just trying to save as many lives as they could. As I was being carried away," he adds, "those same officers were coming down the line in a jeep when their driver hit a landmine. There was a tremendous explosion. The only thing I could make out in the swirl of debris that followed was a wheel from their jeep—spinning around in the air."

While on active duty, Steele found time to complete his high school education, with the help of his Stoneville High School principal. In his absence, his diploma was awarded to his high school sweetheart, Mabel Martin. The couple married on February 7, 1944. They have two daughters, Jane and Jinx.

Steele worked at various jobs for a few years: farming, clerking in a grocery store, driving a laundry truck. In 1965, he sought employment with the United States Postal Service, his Purple Heart placing him at the head of a line of applicants. He carried mail on a Stoneville route for twenty-five years before retiring. He remains an active member of the Stoneville community.

Russell Stewart

*We were hit by a big wave coming off another ship. Our ship
was suspended in air and literally cracked in the middle.*

"I was in combat waters for thirty-five months, and I never
fired a shot," marvels former Navy gunner's mate third
class Russell Stewart. "That's one thing I don't have on my
conscience. I never killed anyone."

Stewart joined the Navy in May 1943. Before he took his basic training
at Great Lakes, Illinois, he had never seen the ocean. "First time I went
out on the water, I was scared to death," he acknowledges. He adapted
quickly, however, and was eventually shipped to Little Creek, Virginia,
where he was trained as a Navy armed guard, assigned to protect merchant
ships. These civilian-owned vessels, operated by steamship lines, were
not designed to withstand enemy attack, even when fitted with defensive
weapons. Traditionally, they had not carried armed guards. "It was a
new thing for all of us," Stewart says. "We didn't know what to expect.
England sent destroyer escorts to protect the ships from wolf packs. Still,
they were being sunk as fast as they went on the ocean."

Indeed, according to American Merchant Marine at War (www.
usmm.org/ww2.html.), merchant marines suffered the highest rate of
casualties of any service in World War II. During the war, 1,544 ships
were sunk due to war conditions, and hundreds more were damaged by
torpedoes, bombs, shelling, or kamikaze pilots.

Stewart's first mission was to Liverpool, England. His ship was not
attacked directly during the crossing, but a couple of ships in his fleet

were lost. He says the most dreaded voyages were to Murmansk, Russia, and Antwerp, Belgium, because these were the areas where the largest number of ships had been lost. Nevertheless, after two tours in Liverpool, he received orders to go to Antwerp. "We sailed into Liverpool and sat there and waited. We had to go into the English Channel; that was the only way in, and that was close enough to the Germans that they constantly guarded it with aircraft. We could hear airplanes every time we went in. We would always catch a heavy fog before entering, but still we would lose ships."

After his first trip to Belgium, Stewart was given a short leave. Upon his return, he was ordered back to Belgium, this time aboard a different ship. When he arrived, he saw his former ship and strolled over to talk with the crew. He learned that they had lost men on their voyage but had also shot down two German planes. As Stewart was leaving—he estimates he had gotten about one hundred yards away—he heard a loud explosion. "I froze," he declares, pausing to relive the moment. "At that late stage of the war, the Germans were dropping a large number of buzz bombs and V-2 rockets, especially against British and Belgian targets. Sure enough, one had hit right beside my old ship. The entire superstructure was destroyed; the vessel was lost—along with a number of the crew."

Buzz bombs—also called "doodlebugs"—were early guided missiles. Stewart describes them as "miniature airplanes that run out of gas and just fall out of the sky. If you look up when one is falling, it looks like it is falling right on your head, no matter how far it misses you." V-2 rockets were the first ballistic missiles, the first man-made objects to achieve space flight. Unlike buzz bombs, they appeared out of the stratosphere without warning; they could not be shot down because they could not be spotted.

Eventually, Stewart was ordered back to England. "For the first time, there were infantry soldiers onboard ship. We were all puzzled as to what their presence could mean. To add to the confusion, when we arrived in England, we learned that no shore leaves would be granted. Three days later, we were told that we were being pulled from our current duties to participate in an invasion into France.

"Every day, a specified number of men were removed from the ship to join the invasion forces. On the last day—the day I was supposed to be pulled—I was standing guard duty when suddenly I heard the roar of planes overhead. I looked up to see the air filled with aircraft headed toward France. 'Thank God,' I said to myself. 'It's started, and they missed me.'" Due to adverse weather conditions on the sea, the invasion had taken place one day early. Stewart did not have to go.

He was to make another trip into Belgium, but while the ship was en route, the war in Europe ended. The delighted sailors set sail for the United States. Regrettably, two ships were lost during the return voyage—*after* the war had ended. Stewart was shipped immediately to Shoemaker, California, where he participated in two weeks of amphibious training. He was then put on a troop transport and sent to Pearl Harbor, Hawaii.

Stewart points out that the crew's assignment in Hawaii was to invade and secure the numerous small islands occupied by the Japanese. "But we were on the tail end of the war," he concedes, "and by the time we got there, everything had been secured. Our routine was to land on an island, leave the LST, make sure everything was all right, and reboard the craft. We anchored on one island in the Philippines, where we spent a miserable night in the pouring rain. The next morning, our transport returned to pick us up. I never knew what that was all about."

They sailed to Luzon, set up camp, and stayed about a month. Their instructions were to "mop up"—clear out any remaining Japanese forces. For this action, Stewart received a Battle Star: "I never did think I really deserved it," he shares honestly. "Everything was over when we got there. There *were* Japanese soldiers in the tunnels, but I don't believe their number warranted all the American forces that were there."

When Stewart was sent to Okinawa, he encountered the same situation: his predecessors had done the hard fighting. "The Good Lord was with me all the way," he observes, "although I did get caught on the ocean during a couple of typhoons. Once, I did not get back on land in time to enter the safety bunker and found my tent had blown over. I crawled under the collapsed mass and pulled a mattress over my body. It got so dark I couldn't see a thing. I heard a moan and shouted for the person to identify himself. No response. I believe a Japanese soldier was sharing my tent. I took out my trench knife and held it for the rest of the night. The next morning, I was alone."

Stewart rode out another hurricane in the North Atlantic. "We were hit by a big wave coming off another ship. Our ship was suspended in air and literally cracked in the middle. Crippled, we were forced to leave the safety of our convoy and sail to St. John's, Newfoundland, for repairs. When we got back, the convoy was gone. We followed the coastline around Iceland. Fortunately, we were not attacked, but we almost froze to death."

While in Okinawa, Stewart was part of a fleet preparing to invade Japan. Once again, before the attack occurred, conditions changed: the first atomic bomb fell. His ship anchored just off the Tokyo coastline to "wait and see what was going to happen." Another bomb fell. Not long afterward, the sailors watched the battleship USS *Missouri* arrive in Tokyo Bay. On that ship, on September 2, 1945, the treaty marking the end of World War II was signed. The crew of Stewart's LST unloaded the soldiers and tanks they had on board and went ashore.

Stewart decided to explore an abandoned factory: "I found a gun, a bayonet, and a Japanese flag. When I got back on ship, several Japanese boys came aboard in search of food. I asked one of them to autograph the flag, which he did. To this day, I have no idea what the boy wrote. It may have been his name, or it may have been a curse."

Stewart terminates the interview with the disclosure that from that time forward, he just "messed around" until he accumulated enough points to come home. After his discharge, he returned to his home in Landsberg, Virginia, and went to work for the Mount Airy Knitting Company. He eventually moved to Mount Airy and later to Winston-Salem, where he obtained a job with Reynolds Tobacco Company. He worked for the cigarette manufacturer until he retired. In 1978, he married Inice Nelson and moved to Madison. Stewart has one son, Greg, from a previous marriage.

Fifty-two years after Stewart was discharged from the Navy, US Senator Richard Burr awarded him the World War II Honorable Service Lapel Pen; the World War II Victory Medal; an American Campaign Medal; the European-African-Middle-Eastern Campaign Medal; the Asiatic-Pacific Campaign Medal; the Navy Occupation Service Medal; and the Philippine Liberation Medal.

Lee Donald Tuttle

Bombs were going off everywhere; the noise was deafening.

"Tuttle Returns After Seeing Much Action," proclaimed Lee Donald Tuttle's hometown newspaper regarding his return after five years and six months of historic military service. The "action" to which the headline alluded included helping Lieutenant Colonel James H. "Jimmy" Doolittle prepare his airplane for the legendary Doolittle Raid on Tokyo; participating in the pivotal Battle of Midway; and being rescued from the USS *Hornet* after Japanese torpedoes sank her.

"I was a seventeen-year-old Madison High School student when I persuaded four of my buddies to join me in enlisting in the Navy," says Tuttle. He adds quickly, "All five of us survived the war." This is an astounding statistic, considering five hundred thousand American lives were lost in that conflict.

Tuttle took his basic training in Norfolk, Virginia. He then traveled to Jacksonville, Florida, where he spent four months learning to be an aviation metalsmith. The seaman second class was assigned to the USS *Hornet* (CV 8), an aircraft carrier commissioned at Norfolk on October 20, 1941, with Captain Marc A. Mitscher in command. Unbeknownst to captain or crew, the *Hornet* was about to participate in the most ambitious, daring exploit yet undertaken by the United States in the Pacific War.

After the December 7, 1941, attack on Pearl Harbor, American and Allied personnel were in desperate need of an aerial victory to boost sagging morale. Believing it feasible to launch twin-engine bombers from the deck of an aircraft carrier, General Henry "Hap" Arnold tapped technically savvy Doolittle to organize and lead an air strike on Japanese home islands.

On April 2, 1942, the *Hornet* headed west across the Pacific, with sixteen Army B-25s sitting on her flight deck. Doolittle's plan was to wait until they came within four hundred miles of Japan, launch their aircraft, drop their bomb loads on and around Tokyo, and still have enough fuel to make it to airfields in China. Vice Admiral William F. "Bull" Halsey's flagship *Enterprise* would join them and supply air cover for Doolittle's raiders.

Meanwhile, a portion of Doolittle's cowling flew over the side of the ship. "This was especially bad because cowling helps prevent *drag*—an aerodynamic force that opposes an airplane's motion through the air," explains Tuttle. "Since Doolittle's plane was to be the first off the flight deck—making his takeoff distance shorter than that of the other planes— it was important that he encounter no resistance to early lift. I was called upon to fit and attach new metal around the exposed elevator shaft. But I was taken by surprise when Colonel Doolittle later looked me up to shake my hand and say he appreciated my help."

On April 18, while the *Hornet* was still more than six hundred miles away from target, enemy picket boats spotted the carrier, forcing the pilots to take off earlier than planned. The fuel required to cover the additional two hundred miles lessened the likelihood that they would reach China. Even so, their bombs fell on Tokyo and the surrounding areas, significantly raising confidence in American capabilities and causing deep embarrassment to Japanese high command. All aircraft involved in the mission were lost, and eleven crewmen were killed or captured. Still, most of the eighty pilots and crew, including Doolittle, survived. After the last Army plane became airborne, the *Hornet* crew brought her own planes back on deck and sped away toward Pearl Harbor.

"After the Tokyo Raid," reports Tuttle, "Japan attempted to avoid the risk of further such incidents by eliminating all American aircraft carriers. This led to the Battle of Midway six weeks later." On June 4,

1942, the *Hornet*, the *Yorktown*, and the *Enterprise* launched strikes on Japanese carrier-based planes headed for Midway. In what has been called the "greatest carrier battle in history," the *Hornet*'s famed Torpedo Squadron 8 pressed the attack hard. Met with overwhelming resistance, they continued to pound the enemy until each of their fifteen planes was shot down. Only one pilot survived. Two days later, on June 6, *Hornet* aircraft assisted in damaging or destroying two Japanese cruisers and a destroyer, spelling the beginning of the end for Japanese forces. Japanese carrier strength was crippled, and Midway was saved as a base from which to launch operations into the western Pacific.

Tuttle vividly remembers the Battle of Santa Cruz Island, which took place on October 26, 1942. Until two days earlier, when she was joined by the *Enterprise*, the *Hornet* had guarded the sea approach to the Solomon Islands' Guadalcanal alone. On the morning of the confrontation, planes from the two carriers had bombed and severely disabled several enemy vessels, but the *Hornet* was herself under heavy attack. "Bombs were going off everywhere; the noise was deafening," recalls Tuttle. "The deck was covered with the dead and injured. The damage grew so critical that we finally had to abandon ship."

Recognizing the need for additional nets to be used in the escape, Tuttle rushed to make them available, prompting the chief warrant officer to comment that he had "saved more lives than anyone."

"I was shocked to see Sam Tesh, one of my boyhood friends, among the crew of the USS *Hughes* who came to pick up survivors," observes Tuttle. Together they watched in awe as American destroyers attempted to scuttle the burning *Hornet* to keep her out of enemy hands. But she stubbornly remained afloat until Japanese destroyers fired four 24-inch torpedoes at her flaming hull. One hundred eleven lives were lost, and 108 men sustained injuries.

Remaining *Hornet* crew members were reassigned to the cruiser USS *San Diego*. They docked in New Caledonia—a group of French-speaking islands east of Australia that had been designated a rest and recuperation hospital area for combat troops. "For six weeks, I was assigned to work with Marines who suffered 'shell shock' after the Battle of Guadalcanal," remembers Tuttle. It had taken the Americans an arduous six months to defeat the Japanese in that fiercely contested action.

There were additional stops along the way, but the seamen finally arrived back in the states, where they were given leave. Because all of his belongings had been lost when the *Hornet* sank, Tuttle borrowed money from the Red Cross to purchase a uniform and pay his fare to Madison. While he was at home, his mother decided to clean his uniform—the only one he had—leaving him no choice but to wear civilian clothes when he went into town with friends. Thinking he was AWOL, a local police officer arrested him for being out of uniform. His father intervened to keep him from being carried to jail.

His leave completed, Tuttle carried out various assignments in California, Kansas, Florida, and Virginia. He sums up the remainder of his time in service thus: "I remained in the Navy an extra six months, for which I was paid the grand total of three hundred dollars. I came home a third class petty officer."

On July 9, 1950, Tuttle married Peggy Cardwell of Mayodan. They have three children, Britt, Vicki Wall, and Dee Evans. Tragically, Dee, a psychologist with Rockingham Country Mental Health Clinic, was accidentally killed in 1981, when she slipped on ice.

Now retired from the neighborhood grocery store they formerly owned and operated, the Tuttles make their home in Mayodan.

Robert "Bobby" Walker

*People came out of their homes to cheer
and applaud as we passed by.*

It was 1954. Eisenhower was president, and the country was enmeshed in the Korean Conflict. But closer to home, in Phenix City, Alabama—mecca for a powerful crime syndicate—martial law was being declared for the only time in American history other than for riots or natural disasters. GIs stationed a few miles north of the city at Fort Benning, Georgia, were drawn to the clubs, gambling halls, and houses of prostitution, where they became easy targets for unscrupulous dealers. They often had their money stolen, or worse, were beaten or killed.

When local businessman Hugh Bentley sought to organize the community to fight crime, his house was bombed. His friend Albert Patterson was elected attorney general on an anti-crime platform and was immediately gunned down in the street. The National Guard was called in, as were military policemen (MPs) from Fort Bragg, one of them being Bobby Walker of Eden. Walker and his comrades patrolled the streets, raided gambling institutions, burned illicit equipment, and assisted in bringing more than seven hundred perpetrators to justice.

"There was no doubt in my mind that the residents of the city wanted us to be there," insists Walker. "As I led military convoys across the bridge into the area where they were to bivouac, people came out of their houses to cheer and applaud as we passed by."

Walker graduated Leaksville High School and was working for Fieldcrest Mills of Eden when he was drafted in August 1953. He went through basic training at Fort Jackson, South Carolina, and then traveled to Camp Gordon, Georgia, where he was selected and trained for duty with the military police. Afterward, he moved to Fort Bragg, his home base for the duration of his term.

A motorcycle enthusiast since age sixteen, Walker was appropriately assigned to patrol the area and escort convoys of visiting dignitaries via his motorbike. As MP, he was also called on to investigate reports of disturbances or disorderly conduct on base. On one such occasion, he was dispatched to the home of a lieutenant, where a party had apparently gotten out of hand. The lieutenant was away, and his wife was not happy at being reprimanded. "She walked up to me and *slapped* me across the face," he laments, still exhibiting shock. The corporal maintained his dignity, however, and eventually made her understand that she and her guests needed to lower the noise level or disband the party.

Prior to helping restore order in Phenix City, Fort Bragg MPs were assigned to patrol the streets—this time in jeeps—during 1954's category three Hurricane Hazel, one of the most destructive storms in North Carolina history. Battling fifty-mile-per-hour winds, torrential rains, and heavy flooding, the soldiers searched for stranded or injured motorists, while keeping their eyes peeled for looters and vandals preying on vacated property.

Walker completed his military service in January 1955, returned to Eden, married, and found employment with Fieldcrest, Karastan, and finally DuPont, where he remained twenty-four years. He retired early to care for his ailing wife, Louise, who suffered from Parkinson's disease. She passed away in 2000, leaving behind not only her husband of forty years, but also four adult children.

In 2001, Walker married Jewel Almond, a widow with whom he had been friends before either of their first marriages. The couple currently lives in Stoneville, where, on sunny days, they may be spotted streaming down the highway on their motorcycle built for two.

William E. "Bouse" Williams

People were screaming; whistles were blowing;
someone kept yelling, "We've been hit!"

The year 1938 will be remembered for many things: Teflon was invented; the New York Yankees swept the Cubs in four straight games to win the World Series; Superman made his debut via Action Comics; Spencer Tracy won Best Actor for *Boys Town*; Orson Welles generated widespread panic with his radio dramatization of H. G. Wells's classic novel *War of the Worlds*; Adolph Hitler was named *Time* magazine's Man of the Year. But when Germany invaded Czechoslovakia, Bouse Williams could smell American involvement in war.

Not comfortable with the idea of being drafted, the Mayodan man drove to Danville, Virginia, and enlisted in the Navy. Weighing in at a mere 129 pounds, Williams questioned whether he would be accepted. "No problem. I was sworn in, transported to Norfolk, fitted with military issue, and assigned a bunk before 9:00 p.m. the same day. Then I was herded into the mess hall—which smelled like dirty dishrags—and fed supper. That night, I dreamed of joining the Navy and woke up asking, 'How do I get out of this place?'"

After thirteen weeks of boot camp, Williams came home on leave and married his sweetheart, Madge Bryant of Stuart, Virginia. Before they knew it, he was boarding a train for Long Beach, California, where he joined the crew of the USS *Pennsylvania*. The battleship was engaged in fleet tactics and battle maneuver procedures around Hawaii and the

Caribbean Sea. He became a gunner's mate second class. In 1939, the ship was sent to Pearl Harbor. "Just three weeks before I was supposed to be discharged, on December 7, 1941, the Japanese bombed Pearl Harbor. I had to stay in the Navy an additional three years, eight months, and ten days."

The USS *Pennsylvania* was moored within dry dock #1—adjacent to Ford Island—to have her shafts and propellers aligned. Williams was in the ship's armory drinking coffee with a former Marine when he heard a loud noise and felt the ship quake. "What was that?" he asked.

"Sounded like a damn bomb to me!" replied his companion.

Williams started outside to investigate. "When I raised my foot to step out of the hatch, another bomb hit. People were screaming; whistles were blowing; someone kept yelling, 'We've been hit!' I immediately pictured my two brothers fighting in North Africa. 'What is going to happen to them?' Then I thought about my mother. 'She will be so worried.'" Williams's attention was jarred back to the present crisis when he heard men yelling for ammunition. "I had the keys to the ammunition magazine," he remembered. "I ran to unlock the room."

Williams was originally assigned to an antiaircraft gun, but when a gunner's mate first class wanted to go on deck and get some air, he used his rank to claim Williams's position. Williams was reassigned to a turret. During air raids, men assigned to turrets left their posts to form supply lines for antiaircraft gunners. When the bomb hit, the electric supply line was damaged, so they were forced to use chain horses to get shells to the gunners. "The gunners were shooting faster than the backup supply line could run," explains Williams. Shouts of "pass the ammunition" resounded throughout the ship. "While I was running around trying to distribute ammunition, I passed the antiaircraft gun I would have been firing. The only part left of the guy who pulled rank on me was his right arm."

The USS *Pennsylvania* was one of the first to open fire as enemy dive and torpedo bombers roared out of the overcast sky. Although spared destruction, she was hit with a bomb on her starboard deck, crippling a five-inch gun and killing its crew. The battleship was severely strafed and pelted with flying fragments, while oil fires from other ships moored in dry dock damaged her bow. Williams speaks fondly of a crane operator who likely prevented further damage and loss of life by moving his crane up and down the dock, swinging a huge ball protectively back and forth over the ship.

The attack came in three waves. After the first, Williams went topside to assess the damage. He watched, stunned, as the USS *Nevada* ran ashore and the USS *Oklahoma* turned over. Amid the chaos, he saw sailors walking around dazed—obviously suffering shell shock—and survivors from destroyed vessels struggling to climb over the sides of his ship. Fire had ignited when a shell exploded next to one of the magazines.

Williams was instructed to remove explosives from the ammunition room to prevent further destruction. Before he could carry out his orders, he had to displace the bodies of two men killed in the blast. "I took two burlap bags and literally shoveled their body pieces into the bags—alternating shovelfuls into first one and then the other. I put a dog tag in each bag. Apparently, someone had already thrown the heads overboard; they were never found."

While delivering ammunition to be tossed over the side, Williams spotted a hand severed from its body. He had to pass by it three or four times as he walked back and forth. He determined that on his next passage, he would throw it overboard. When he paused to carry out his mission, however, it was gone. "I could not get the image of that hand out of my mind," he says. "It haunted me. Later, while performing patrol duty on third deck, I walked out of one compartment and started around a corner. A sailor sleeping on the bottom bunk had his hand lying on the floor beside him. A shaft of light coming through the door was shining on it, making it look for the world like it was detached from his body. When I came on it unexpectedly, it scared me so bad I hit it with my billy club. The poor sailor screamed, and the entire crew jumped up and manned their battle stations. *That's* how nervous we all were."

The attack lasted from 7:55 a.m. until approximately 11:00 a.m., but the sailors had to remain at their posts for thirty hours. When it was over, fifteen crewmen were dead, including the executive officer; fourteen were missing in action; and thirty-eight were wounded. "I was too busy to be afraid during the attack," admits Williams, "but afterward, while we were confined to our stations, I was terrified that the Japanese planes would return. When time permitted, I got all my belongings ready to be sent home. 'This war is going to go on,' I reasoned, 'and the way they hit us this day, I'm not going to live through it.'"

Overall, the number of American souls lost on Pearl Harbor that morning was 2,403—two-thirds of them killed during the first fifteen minutes of battle, when the USS *Oklahoma*, USS *Utah*, and USS *Arizona* were bombed. In contrast, fifty-five Japanese airmen died.

One of Williams's scariest moments came after the fighting was over. He and two others were commanded to take a boat to the ammo dump buried on the other side of the island to obtain additional supplies. "I *knew* that at any minute those planes were going to come back and catch us out there in open water." Thankfully, that did not happen, and they were able to complete their mission. Williams was promoted to gunner's mate first class.

As a result of the attack on Pearl Harbor, angry Americans volunteered to enter the military in droves. The rallying cry became "Remember Pearl Harbor." Admiral Yamamoto Isoroku, architect of the Japanese attack, is said to have lamented that a "sleeping giant" had been awakened.

Three weeks after the attack on Pearl Harbor, the crew of the USS *Pennsylvania* learned that they were going to shift berths (relocate). They ended up in Long Beach, California, where the ship underwent repairs. Williams was in San Francisco about three months. Madge joined him. It was during this time that their first daughter, Bonnie Williams Connelly, was conceived. (They also had a second child, Cynthia, who died of an aneurysm at age thirty-two.) Madge returned home when Williams was transferred to the naval base in Washington, DC, to attend gunnery school. There he would spend three months studying electric hydraulics.

After gunnery school, he was sent to Recife, Brazil, aboard the USS *Memphis*—a four-stack cruiser with no hydraulic equipment. For the next two years, his assignment was to patrol for submarines between Brazil and North Africa. Eventually, Williams was brought back to San Francisco for reassignment as captain on an attack transport ship. The war ended before that could take place. One month later, after seven years, eight months, and ten days of active duty, Williams earned enough points to come home. He accepted a job with Sears & Roebuck in Greensboro.

William E. "Bouse" Williams, ninety-one, died on Tuesday, November 17, 2009. His wife preceded him in death one year earlier on November 28, 2008. They had been married seventy years.

Alexander Worth

*Americans ... were dragged, unprepared, feet first, and
screaming, into the second global war of the century.*

I am ringing the doorbell of retired Ranger Alexander Worth's
luxurious Well Spring apartment in Greensboro, tape recorder in
hand. I guess I am expecting a cynical, battle-hardened, Patton
look-alike to appear. Instead, an attractive, soft-spoken gentleman,
exuding charm and ease of manner, greets me. We become instant
friends, and he agrees not only to an interview but also to appear as
special guest for God Bless America Day, a Fourth of July celebration
sponsored by Woodbine Baptist Church in nearby Mayodan.

Worth, a Durham native, graduated from the Citadel, the Military
College of South Carolina, in 1940, earning the prestigious Light Infantry
Saber award, signifying excellence in military techniques and strategy.
Hitler was already on the march in Europe, and Worth, like most of his
classmates, enlisted in the Army. In 1942, he was sent to Europe, attached
to the Eighth Bomber Command, and in January 1943, he became part
of a defense unit relocating to North Africa.

Meanwhile, Colonel William Darby (posthumously promoted to
general) and his Rangers had just returned from the Tunisian campaign.
The colonel set about expanding his Ranger units to three battalions:
First, Third, and Fourth. When the call went out for volunteers, Worth
could hardly wait to get to Darby's headquarters and sign up. Because of
his advanced military training, superb physical condition, and enthusiasm

for the task, he was selected—making him the first Citadel graduate to be tapped for the Rangers.

"This was a special combat unit," he explains, "consisting entirely of volunteers for hazardous duty, the forerunners of today's special operations forces." Worth, a captain, became commander of Fox Company, First Battalion, Darby's Rangers, directing a unit of sixty men on risky assignments in Sicily and Italy.

The following excerpts are taken from Worth's personal memoirs, written June 6, 1984, for his three sons, their wives, and subsequent descendants. He begins by stating, "I will not vouch for the accuracy of *all* the events recorded here since, after all, they are being put down on paper more than forty years after the fact … The remarks are intended purely as a record of my own personal experiences as I recall them."

Sicily

I was company commander of Fox Company, First Battalion, and our sector of beach was about four hundred feet wide. On our right flank sector was an enemy machine gun inside a small, stone, fisherman's hut. To the left flank was a concrete machine gun "pillbox" especially made to defend a path leading up to the little fishing village of Gela, which sat on a bluff probably about forty feet above sea level.

We were to knock out the two protected machine guns in our sector, ascend the bluff, fight our way through the town (only two or three city blocks) and "dig in" defensive positions on the north side of town. There we were to prepare to defend against an expected enemy counterattack designed to force us back into the sea.

I stepped off the ramp into hip deep water just behind my lead scout ... The air was thick with rifle, machine gun, and mortar fire. We had been trained to run onto the beach. I distinctly recall how it felt as if I were moving through chewing gum in slow motion. I ran straight toward a little tidal drainage slough, which I had seen in the photos, instinctively crouching to present a small target, and froze suddenly in my tracks just inches away from a trip wire which was elevated about six inches above ground level by pins stuck in the sand. The wire was attached to mines buried in the sand. If I tripped the wire the mines would detonate ... I stepped over it gingerly and moved toward the right flank machine gun.

A mortar shell landed very close to my left, and I felt a severe impact on my left knee, but no pain.

Up the path we scrambled single file and into the streets of the village [machine guns having been eliminated]. There we saw enemy soldiers running away in every direction ... We walked ... to our final objective on the outer perimeter of Gela and dug our foxholes to prepare for an expected counteroffensive.

While the enemy troops continued the march toward us in battle formation ... three rounds were fired from the cruiser two miles out at sea, almost instantly three more, until probably twenty or more salvos had been fired ... then the command "Cease fire." ... In a few minutes when the dust had settled, where previously there had been a thousand men, now not one single soul remained. It was awesome, devastating, stupefying, carnage, more than the senses are conditioned to absorb, frightening even to those whose interest was served, a sickening spectacle, which I shall never forget.

Sitting on the side of my foxhole, I glanced down and noticed two neatly sliced "L" shaped holes in my pants leg, rolled up my pants and saw that dried blood covered my knee, thanks to that mortar shell on the beach.

At two hours after midnight sharp, we moved out across the eerie plain ... three companies abreast, about one hundred yards apart ... We had about two and a half hours to cover the estimated four-mile distance to the foot of the mountain range and make a dawn attack at 4:30 a.m.

When we came within three hundred to four hundred yards of the hill, the fury of the "fiery furnace" itself seemed suddenly to be upon us. The front of a haystack on the hillside opened up on hinged doors. The machine guns inside immediately began firing in my direction ... I saw advancing toward me ... a string of innocent little puffs of powder from the earth ... it took me a split moment to react, not recognizing those innocent puffs for what they were—machine gun bullets striking the earth ... I yelled to warn the men behind me and nimbly stepped to one side while the puffs kept marching by, just a foot away ... Then immediately, all down the line instincts and training took over. The first squad redeployed from single file to a line abreast and each man kneeled and began firing his rifle ... My mortar crew hastily set up their weapon and began to lob mortar shells ... Within moments the guns were silenced and the remaining enemy soldiers came out with hands up and waving a white handkerchief.

The relief we felt was only short lived when we were ordered to join "C" Company on a forced march for a dawn attack on the impenetrable mountain fortress of Butera.

There was no attempt at a counterattack at Butera, and "F" Company finally had a day or two of well-deserved rest … Now I began to notice that my knee, which had caught some mortar fragments on the invasion at Gela, was a little sore.

When the company came to the Sicilian town of Caltanissetta—liberated earlier by the First Division—prisoners were turned over to Worth, who was also ordered to govern the town until Amgot (Allied Military Government for Occupied Territories) could get there. He released a town council member, imprisoned by the fascists as an alleged communist sympathizer, upon learning that she held a degree in civil management. "All day long, I sat at the mayor's desk," he notes, "with my communist deputy and interpreter at my side, and listened to the complaints and proposals." Order was maintained and most complaints resolved. Amgot arrived two days later.

On one occasion, Colonel Darby surprised Worth by asking, "How much do you know about mules?"

"I think I could tell the difference between the front and the rear of one," he replied.

"Well, I've got a job for you … I want you to organize a mule supply train to provide food, water, and four 75 mm. pack cannons with ammunition for the operation."

"Yes Sir, Sir," called Worth, executing a first-class salute. Having a few men who spoke "mule," he authorized the supply sergeant to liberate thirty or forty mules from the surrounding farms, issuing each owner an IOU stating that the United States Army owed him the price of one mule. Soon F Company's mule train was loaded and ready to go. Worth describes the following incidents in his memoirs:

> One day as I walked alongside my mule on the downslope side of a hill, we received machine gun fire from nearby upslope. I took close cover behind my mule. I heard some dull thuds as the bullets struck somewhere close to me. Suddenly the little mule just toppled over and rolled down the hillside with all his luggage strapped to his back.
>
> Occasionally we passed through small villages. Then the villagers came out to greet us with broad smiles and showing their affection and relief with little bunches of wild flowers or fruit. To live up to my role as conquering hero, I requisitioned a real horse to replace my lost mule, in order to ride through in style. At the first village after I acquired the horse, just as we reached a large group of cheering fans, the poor half-starved animal heaved a sigh, fell to his knees, and rolled over on me, where I was pinned until one of the villagers came to my rescue. Such indignity! So much for the role of conquering hero.

Italy

Of course, we felt deep pride, mixed with some little apprehension, in having again been chosen to be the first wave of invasion troops to penetrate the European Continent in force, since Hitler had conquered Poland and France over two years before … British Commandos and our 1st, 3rd, and 4th Ranger Battalions would land several miles north of Salerno, deep inside enemy lines, and attempt to interdict the enemy supply routes ...

Our precise invasion objective was the cove of a small fishing village named Maori on the Sorrento Peninsula ... After the village had been secured, the 1st Battalion would filter through the 4th and move inland for several miles toward an enemy fortified position known as Chiunzi Pass.

We proceeded toward it (our objective) in the dark, twisting frequently around the mountain turns, my scout and I in the lead. What ... should appear ... but a German patrol of several officers, noncoms and armed men. My scout, armed with a carbine, and I with my GI 45 clbre drawn, crept quietly toward them, hugging the hillside closely ... When my scout and I suddenly confronted them, our weapons in their faces, at the very edge of their vehicle, they were so taken by surprise they hesitated just a moment too long to put up a defense ... We captured six of the enemy and not a shot fired to reveal our presence.

... At a range of about one hundred feet, blocking the road were two armored scout cars with heavy machine guns mounted in the turrets and aimed directly at us! Corporal Smith and I, crouching low beneath the tank's gun muzzle, slithered to within about forty feet from the armored vehicle. I loaded his Bazooka with an armor piercing round and said, "I doubt if we'll get a second chance; make it a good one." ... Then suddenly the flash, and the armor piercing round caught the vehicle in its most vulnerable spot ... Screams and moans came from inside ... Sergeant Van Skoy hurried past us up to the stricken vehicle and dropped a fragmentation grenade inside … the moaning and the crying stopped. I didn't like it.

"F" Company had achieved its assigned point guard mission successfully without a single friendly casualty.

Captain Worth was awarded a citation for leading and expediting the successful assault and march to Chiunzi Pass. His memoirs continue as follows:

> After weeks of holding off the enemy in the hills of the Sorrento Peninsula, we received orders to join the main force of 5th Army for a breakout to Naples some twenty miles to the northwest. The back of the German resistance was finally broken as they retreated to form new defensive positions north of Naples. Resistance was light and we entered the beleaguered city about the end of September. The Rangers were placed in reserve to prepare for another day.

Worth's injured knee had grown progressively worse. Finally on training status, he decided to report to sick call at the US Army Hospital in Naples. He was carrying shrapnel. His leg was placed in a cast from hip to ankle. "When the cast was removed," he confesses, "I slipped out of the hospital to return to my unit, which had been sent to active duty in the Venafro sector just north of Naples. Ranger Colonel Bill Martin picked me up on the road to Venafro and drove me back to the hospital with instructions to 'stay put until officially discharged.' I was sent to a hospital near Bizerte in North Africa to recuperate. While I was there, the First Battalion was annihilated in an ill-conceived attempt to break out of the Anzio beachhead perimeter south of Rome. I never returned to combat and was finally sent home in March of 1944."

The captain sped to the arms of his waiting bride, the former Anne Preston, from whom he had been separated for eighteen months. They had first met at a Citadel dance: "I saw this beautiful girl in an emerald green dress," he confides. "My friend asked if I wanted to meet her. 'Damn right!' I shot back." They married on February 3, 1942, and remained sweethearts until her death on November 3, 1990. They have three sons: Alexander Walker, David McAlister, and Robert Preston.

Worth established Shamrock Corporation in Greensboro, an enterprise currently managed by twin sons David and Robert. In 1992, the Ranger took his second bride, the former Margaret Crowell.

Appendix 1

Major Howard Gurley shared the following letter with the author in 2007. It was written for his family, to convey what World War II fighter pilot missions could entail. Major Gurley was a member of Combat Airmen/ Joshua's Troops until his death on April 15, 2009.

Only One Survivor

One day in early January, 1944, there were five P-47 Thunderbolt pilots meeting in a hospital room in Gravesend, England, near the Thames River, just south of London. This is the story of what brought them together at that bedside and what happened to each of them later during the war. They were all pilots in the 358th Fighter Group, 365th Squadron. Of the five, I was the only one to survive the war. Each of the [other] four was killed in a different way. Their names were Major Frank Ross, our squadron commander; Lieutenant Josef L. Green; Lieutenant Cletus Tusing; and Lieutenant Jay "Herky" Thomson.

We had flown an escort mission December 31, 1943, near Paris, flying from our base in Leiston, England. Being low on fuel, a number of us were just able to get back to England. Lieutenant Green had been injured in a crash landing. To visit Green, Major Ross flew us to a RAF [Royal Air Force] base near Gravesend.

As to what happened to each pilot later, Lieutenant Green was killed flying as an instructor; Lieutenant Tusing was killed on a high altitude mission, diving right to the ground from twenty-five thousand feet. We called him, but got no answer. We believe he had passed out due to an oxygen mask problem. At that altitude, without oxygen, you passed out within twenty to thirty seconds.

Lieutenant Thomson was shot down by German fighters. I was flying with Major Ross April 4, 1944, when we were strafing a German airfield at low level in Normandy. I was flying as his wingman just behind him, when his plane was hit by enemy fire, and I saw it explode. He was killed, never knowing what hit him. I had also been flying on the mission when Tusing and Thomson were lost. We had all trained and flown together. I doubt that any of us in that hospital room would have anticipated that only one of us would be alive at war's end.

Major Howard L. Gurley, USAF, Retired

Appendix 2

Dick Pennstrom, a member of Combat Airmen/Joshua's Troops, wrote this account after he spoke at Bethany Elementary School in Madison.

Bethany Elementary School
Rockingham County, North Carolina

The following story is true and happened about six years ago when I was invited to speak to a kindergarten class at Bethany School in Rockingham County, North Carolina. My granddaughter, Kelley Pruitt, had been speaking with the teacher about her grandfather being a World War Two veteran, who would be willing to speak to the class and answer questions. It so happened that one of her sons, my great grandson Andrew Pruitt, was in the class.

It was a beautiful fall day, not a cloud in the sky, and I arrived while parents in their SUVs and the school buses were delivering children to the drop-off area where the assistant principal and a number of teachers were on bus duty, welcoming the children and guiding them safely into the building. One teacher saw me and recognized the license plate on the front of my car that states "Combat Airman WW-II." She sent three young boys to help me bring my displays and models to the library where they would be set up.

There was coffee, orange juice, and sweet rolls in the cafeteria for the visitors, and then at 9:00 a.m., an official welcome in the gymnasium for the veterans, parents, and children. A well-planned program followed in which children were recognized for their special accomplishments, patriotic music was played, and a demonstration of close order drill was performed by a military team in uniform. The students and the adults all enjoyed it immensely.

Then, the volunteer speakers, such as I, were assigned to classes where we would speak to children and answer questions. I had planned to show a three or four minute silent video of the airplane I flew in combat performing different maneuvers that I would explain to the class. Since these were very young children, I had decided not to speak about firing, or shooting guns, killing people, or anything violent that might scare them, or puzzle them at their early age.

The teacher quietly mentioned to me that, because the children were so young, they might become restless after a few minutes and get up from their places on the floor and wander around the room. She explained that I should not feel badly, or insulted. It was simply that their attention span was quite different from that of an adult. I responded that I completely understood and would not be offended in the least.

So, with that in mind, I started the video and explained what was happening with every maneuver. The students were entranced and watched silently. Then, when the tape was finished, they asked all kinds of questions about the plane, about how I felt as I made the plane do the various maneuvers, and did I ever get sick, like on a roller coaster. To the question of sickness I answered honestly. "No! Not as long as I was doing the flying." I added that I had gotten sick on a very few times when someone else was flying and the plane was being bounced around violently in a storm.

So, continuing with my presentation I said, "Now, I'm going to tell you about something I saw the very first time I flew my airplane up to forty-two thousand feet above the earth that no one in this room has ever seen except me. It was higher at that time than *any other plane* in the whole world had ever flown."

"Can anyone guess what it was I saw? Remember it was a cold, clear day just like today. There were no clouds at all and, when I looked out straight in front of me, what did I see?" There were all kinds of guesses, but no one guessed correctly, so I said, "I saw that Christopher Columbus was right!"

"Who is Christopher Columbus?" they yelled.

I answered, "He was one of the first sailors who said he could sail around the world without falling off. Back in those years, most people thought that the world was flat, and if they sailed out into the ocean from Spain, they would fall off the edge of the Earth.

"Well, when I was up that high, about eight miles above the surface of the earth, I could see that the earth was round, that when I looked off and to the left and to the right, the horizon of the earth was indeed curved, and that meant that the earth was round. But," I added, "I also saw something else that surprised me. Can anyone guess what that was?"

And, of course, the children had all kinds of guesses including the sun, the moon, other planets, birds, and so forth, but none knew the real answer. So, I told them. "I looked straight up above me and in the middle of the day with the sun shining brightly down on the earth I saw the stars."

Naturally, they almost all said simultaneously, "How come?"

So, I explained about the sunlight shining down on the oceans of the earth and the light being reflected from the surface of the water up into the sky. And then, how the moisture in the air we breathe, the tiny, tiny water droplets and water vapor (something like steam—invisible water) reflect the light back down onto the earth.

"But," I said, "when I was up that high, there were not enough water droplets to reflect the sun back to earth. The reason for that is that as we go higher up into the sky there is less and less air until there is no air at all. There was no air for me to breathe. That was why I had to have an oxygen mask with tanks of oxygen in my plane for me to breathe. And … there was nothing up that high around me in the air to reflect the sun into my eyes that could blind me. So … that's why when I looked straight up I could see the stars in the middle of the day."

"Wow!" they responded.

Questions and discussions continued until finally the teacher had to interrupt us and say, "Children, it's time for us to go out to recess and time for Mr. Pennstrom to go to the other classes to speak to them." They all thanked me and shook my hand and said they really liked my stories.

Incidentally, thirty-five minutes had elapsed and not one child had gotten up from where he or she sat, and not one wandered around the classroom.

Second Lieutenant Dick Pennstrom, USAF, Retired

Appendix 3

This article is printed with permission of the authors of Taking the Long Way Home. Tom Williams is a member of Combat Airmen/Joshua's Troops. The author is his wife, Mollie.

Tom's Story

His life in the 1930s was not much different from others in the small mill town where he grew up. He led an unexciting, sheltered life. He was reared in a home where each sibling had to work in order to earn money to contribute to the family's survival. Before dawn, regardless of the elements, he—at nine years of age—walked a route around town delivering newspapers. On his school lunch hours, he carried his mother's home cooked meals to employees at a local textile mill. He was an avid baseball fan and enjoyed playing baseball at school and later with the town league. He loved his hometown, Mayodan, a small town in North Carolina, and never ventured very far.

That is, until July 1943. That was when Tom Williams, at eighteen, left home to serve his country. World War II had been declared on December 7, 1941, and Uncle Sam decided it was time for Tom to see the world while defending our country. The first leg of his trip was Camp Cross, South Carolina, where he was sworn into the United States Navy. He was then sent to Chicago for eight weeks of basic training. This was Tom's first time away from Mayodan, and there in Chicago, he became homesick.

After basic training, Tom was granted a one-week leave to come home before being sent into battle. He took great pleasure in the love and support of the people back home, but too soon he had to return to Chicago. From Chicago, Tom and his fellow servicemen rode a train to Norfolk, Virginia, where he was assigned duty on a minesweeper, the U.S.S. Osprey AM 56. After sailing to Texas and Bermuda, the Osprey headed for England. Tom was appointed fireman. His responsibilities included overseeing the water supply, purifying it for drinking. He was also a loader for a twenty-millimeter gun.

En route, his ship stopped at the Azores Islands and from there sailed to England, sweeping for mines. Eventually, the ship headed for Normandy Beach in France, arriving about 6:00 p.m. on June 5, 1944. The sailors' duties were to protect the waters from mines and guard the beach from the enemy. This was in preparation for other military divisions to advance on Normandy Beach the next day, June 6, 1944—D-day. The military plan was to drive back the Germans who had overtaken France.

The sea was teeming with ships. In the sky, airplanes continuously flew reconnaissance over the battle-inflamed area. Tom and two other midshipmen were on deck while their ship scouted for mines. Glad to be on sea rather than on land where bloody battles were taking place, Tom mentioned to his fellow sailors, "Aren't you glad we are on a ship?" Just as he uttered those words, a ball of fire blew directly into their faces. Tom was knocked to the deck and his two comrades were mortally wounded. Tom's head, arms and hands were burned so badly that he described his body as one big blister. He passed out. When he regained consciousness, he ran to the rear of the ship where he waited in excruciating pain—hoping for rescue. Before long, a ship pulled alongside the minesweeper and transferred the Osprey survivors to its deck. All aboard watched the Osprey sink. The next day, wounded sailors were moved onto an LST and transported to a hospital in Liverpool, England.

Tom was hospitalized for several weeks while being treated for his injuries: severe burns, nerve trauma, impaired vision. After he recuperated enough to travel, he was sent to Glasgow, Scotland, where he caught a ship back to the United States. At Lido Beach, New York, Tom boarded a ship to Norfolk, Virginia. On November 11, 1944, he was awarded a Purple Heart medal for his bravery and was medically discharged from military duty.

Tom said that after the battle was over, he was terrified and tense, but interestingly enough, while it was going on, he wasn't afraid. He just did what he had to do and felt fortunate that he was not a part of the 400,000 men who lost their lives during that historical war. Tom was glad to be home—far from the war's desolation.

I am grateful to Tom and all veterans of World War II, who risked their lives so that America can remain a land of peace and freedom.

Mollie Williams

Appendix 4

Earnest Jones is a member of Combat Airmen/Joshua's Troops. Elmer Jones is Earnest's brother and is featured in the following article, written by Elmer's son. Reprinted by permission from Air Force Magazine, published by the Air Force Association.

The Longest Mission

By Charles A. Jones

The crew of the B-29 Double Trouble had some odd moments on a flight fraught with dangers.

In June 1945, Japanese wartime propaganda broadcasts announced that a lone USAAF B-29 bomber had been shot down over Hokkaido, the northernmost of Japan's main islands. The claims surprised the crew aboard the B-29 *Double Trouble*, which was the lone Superfortress on that particular mission.

Double Trouble had safely returned to its base on Guam after flying what is believed to be the longest nonstop combat mission of World War II. The photoreconnaissance mission, flown over the two-day period of June 25–26, covered a staggering 4,650 miles and took 23 hours to complete.

This flight was mission No. 15 for a crew that would eventually be credited with 29 combat sorties. Mission 15 was to conduct radar photographic reconnaissance over various cities in northern Japan.

Double Trouble was manned by Crew P-10 in the 39th Bomb Group, 314th Bomb Wing, XXI Bomber Command. Her officers were all lieutenants: aircraft commander 1st Lt. Thomas A. Bell, pilot 2nd Lt. Richard D. Harrison, navigator 2nd Lt. Joseph F. Callaghan, bombardier 1st Lt. Richard D. Baldridge Jr., and radar observer and instrument specialist 2nd Lt. Elmer C. Jones, the author's father. The enlisted crew comprised flight engineer MSgt. George W. Beaver Jr., radio operator SSgt. David Schulman, central fire controller gunner TSgt. John J. Essig, left gunner SSgt. David E. Potters, right gunner SSgt. Ralph W. Johnson, and tail gunner Sgt. Thomas F. Smith Jr.

Diaries were forbidden for security reasons, but tail gunner Smith kept one with two entries concerning the mission. Under a list headed "Important Dates" is, "15th Mission: 6-26-45 Hokkaido! 23 1/2 hrs."

Smith's diary indicates that the crew briefed at 2:30 p.m. and departed at 5:05 p.m., flying up "without a hitch—fine weather."

In light of the ban on diaries, Jones was more discreet, and documented his missions in small handwritten charts on the blank pages of his "G.I." New Testament. The longest mission was listed as "Radar Photo."

Jones' "Mickey Operator's Flimsy," which also gave details of the mission, also survives.

For security purposes, the radar and the radar observer were both called "Mickey" (after Mickey Mouse) to conceal from the Japanese the B-29's capability to bomb by radar, especially at night. Mickey sat just ahead of the tail gunner, but had no window at his station. This confined environment later led Jones to comment, "I was in the war, but I didn't see the war."

The "flimsy" was a document prepared for Mickey for each mission. It listed the targets on Hokkaido—the cities of Muroran, Sapporo, and Otaru—and also provided directions and Identification Friend or Foe (IFF) system data. Jones, as Mickey, also had some responsibility for the IFF, to prevent attack by friendly forces.

Lights On

Smith wrote that the crew "got some damned good pictures" but that the camera "screwed up" after the second run. He noted that "Lt. Jones used hand camera—but results aren't assured."

P-10 encountered no enemy opposition over Hokkaido, and in fact was inadvertently welcomed by the Japanese when they flew over the airfield at Sapporo that night.

"The unsuspecting Japanese turned on their landing strip lights as the plane circled their field in preparation for another run on [a] target," reported *The Blockbuster*, the 39th Bomb Group's newsletter in Guam, adding that this relieved "the monotony of the trip."

Jones, who did not see Sapporo's lights since he was monitoring the radar screen, heard the announcement over the airplane's intercom that the Sapporo airfield had turned on its landing lights. He suspects that the Japanese—never contemplating B-29 flights so far north over Japan— thought that *Double Trouble* was a Japanese aircraft preparing to land, and thus turned on the landing lights to aid its arrival.

The Sapporo incident provided comic relief for a mission fraught with numerous potential dangers.

As with any mission, *Double Trouble* could have crashed anywhere, anytime. Takeoff and landing mishaps, fighters, anti-aircraft fire, weather, and mechanical malfunctions—all posed hazards.

Parachuting over water or ditching were other dangers, given the size of the Pacific and the risk involved in hitting the water.

Smith's diary, for instance, noted how the bomb group's Crew 13 had been forced to bail out on a regular formation mission with Col. George W. Mundy, the group commander, aboard. "All got out OK," Smith wrote, but this was partly because "Crew 5 escorted them to a sub." When formations flew missions, ships and subs often lined the flight route to retrieve aviators who ditched or parachuted.

P-10 was on a single-ship mission, would have no such assistance, and as Jones described flying over the Pacific, "Boy, that's a huge place."

The emergency or alternate landing site was in Vladivostok in the USSR. "Fortunately we did not have to go there," said Jones, even before word leaked out in the media that the Soviet Union was detaining American servicemen who diverted to Vladivostok. "Of course, we didn't want to go there because if you got interned there, you never got out."

If the crew had to ditch or parachute over the water, it would be without ship or submarine "lifeguards." Jones put it succinctly: "We were on our own."

With no aerial refueling, P-10 had to be self-sufficient. Jones estimated that *Double Trouble* had approximately 8,000 gallons of fuel, including three extra tanks in the bomb bay.

While the old saying about safety in numbers was true for formation flying, flying alone paradoxically also provided a measure of safety for the single-ship missions.

Half a Pint of Fuel

"The Japs, while a strange lot by Western standards, are not dumb," stated an account in the language of the day in *Brief*, an official wartime publication of the United States Army Strategic Air Forces. The article explained that single B-29s were conducting photographic reconnaissance missions over Japan to obtain photographs that formations of B-29s could later use when bombing Japan.

The Japanese knew exactly why a single B-29 was overhead. They knew what it was doing, tracked its path, and submitted detailed reports. They also knew that formations of attacking bombers would eventually follow.

Lone bombers therefore benefited from a degree of protection and were not sitting ducks. Not only did the Japanese defenders want to track the aircraft's path, but the Japanese typically did not fire at single aircraft because doing so would reveal their anti-aircraft gun positions.

Two other dangers were fatigue and fuel consumption. Smith felt the fatigue even while he "enjoyed" the ride. Jones commented on getting "so tired that you can't hardly sleep."

To conserve fuel, the crew flew at "Dear John" speed—197 mph, Smith wrote.

"Dear John" was of course the term for a letter to a service member, ending a romantic relationship. Jones later speculated that Smith, after considering P-10's situation (single ship) and slow speed, knew that if anything went wrong, the mission would end adversely—just as a Dear John letter ended a relationship. "You get a 'Dear John' letter," Jones explained, "and it's all over."

According to the tail gunner's diary, *Double Trouble* eventually landed with just a half-pint of fuel remaining.

The crew was "tired as dogs" by the time it came in at 4:30 p.m. the following day, wrote Smith, but had "a field day over Hokkaido!" At times it "was bright as hell when we were over Jap territory."

"Cities, towns, industrial targets, steel plants," airfields, all were lit up "like Christmas," wrote Smith, who clearly enjoyed the mission. "Circled an airfield as tho [sic] we were back in Kansas! Fun? I never enjoyed myself more. Not one burst of flak—one searchlight, but it went right out.

Navigation lights on coast all on! No blackout. Damn fools we are for even going near the place! Made two runs on one city—big as life!"

Double Trouble returned safely, notwithstanding the Japanese announcement that the "lone B-29" had been shot down over Hokkaido.

The crew had "volunteered" for the mission, although Bell, the pilot and aircraft commander, may have volunteered without bothering to consult the other crewmen in the process. P-10 also had a good radar (the AN/APQ-13), which allowed Jones to obtain excellent radar photographs.

The set was not without its problems, however. It was complicated, difficult to operate, and essentially impossible to fix if broken. "I couldn't repair it even if it was on the ground," said Jones.

Radar bombing results from early 1945 were not coming back as effective as expected, so an expert from the Massachusetts Institute of Technology was flown to the Pacific to examine the problem. He flew thousands of miles to Guam, and flew with the bomb group on some missions, but was ultimately only able to offer a simple "fix" to the radar accuracy problem. He told the radar operators to decrease the "gain" on their radar scopes, thus dimming the target image.

For security reasons, the mission was kept secret until after the Japanese agreed to surrender terms in August 1945.

"It has now been revealed that the B-29 *City of Maywood* [another name for *Double Trouble*] made the longest flight on record," reported an A2 (intelligence) news summary from XXI Bomber Command on Aug. 23, 1945. The B-29 "flew from Guam to Hokkaido and returned, a distance of 4,650 miles, in a few minutes under 23 hours."

Four members of Crew P-10 received Distinguished Flying Crosses through General Orders No. 44 of Aug. 25, 1945 for the mission. They were: aircraft commander Bell, navigator Callaghan, flight engineer Beaver, and radar observer Jones.

The DFC citation chronicles the flight, stating that the crew volunteered for "a highly successful reconnaissance mission," in what it described as "one of the longest combat flights in history." (Other sources, however, state that it was the longest combat flight in history up to that time.)

"A camera malfunction required that a part of the route be retraced so that pictures could be taken with hand cameras," read the DFC citation. "In spite of these obstacles, however, photographs of superior quality and great usefulness were obtained. Throughout this exceptionally long flight, there were constantly present with the lone B-29 dangers from hostile fighters and anti-aircraft defenses, weather, and mechanical malfunctions."

The story of the mission was front-page news for the Sept. 1, 1945 edition of *The Blockbuster.*

It reported that "censorship forbade earlier coverage of this historic nonstop flight, but the honor for it is purely local." *The Blockbuster* reported that *Double Trouble*'s crew spent three hours, 10 minutes flying over Hokkaido.

A *Stars and Stripes* article noted that the flight distance of 4,650 miles is the same as between New York City and Moscow.

The DFC citation mentioned the actions of three of the recipients specifically. Callaghan was cited for navigation skill that enabled the flight to be flown "exactly as briefed"; Beaver for his management of the fuel supply, which had been "closely calculated"; and Jones for obtaining important and much needed reconnaissance photographs.

Long before the lights came on at Sapporo for *Double Trouble,* each of her crew members was highly trained and then assembled to comprise Crew P-10.

The Role of Luck

Although Jones had been drafted into the Army, he wanted no part of ground combat after seeing the movie "All Quiet on the Western Front." He therefore applied for and was accepted into the aviation cadet program, and was later assigned to navigation training.

Each officer, upon commissioning as a second lieutenant, was assigned to a specific corps or branch within the Army. After graduating from navigation school, Jones was appointed a second lieutenant in the Air Corps of the Army of the United States. He had the military occupational specialty of navigator, and later attained the radar observer MOS.

By way of complex training and certification programs such as this, each airman found himself assigned to Crew P-10.

After the 23-hour mission, two more months and 14 missions passed before the crew learned about Japan's August acceptance of surrender terms. They got the news while returning from their 29th and last combat mission.

Under "Important Dates" in Smith's diary is the note, "Japs Give Up!!!"

The crew's 30th and last mission was over the battleship *Missouri*, after the surrender ceremonies in Tokyo Bay.

Jones attributes P-10's survival during 29 long and dangerous combat sorties to Bell's piloting skills and to the Japanese policy of not shooting at single aircraft. Approximately half of P-10's missions were single-ship flights.

Jones, as an expert poker player, also acknowledged the role of luck in the "deadly game" of war. "If you won, you were OK," he later said. "If you lost, you were dead."

Crew P-10 never assembled for a reunion, and time took its toll. As central fire controller Essig wrote in 2000, "Old P-10 crew is getting smaller every year."

Today, Jones is P-10's only survivor—even the aircraft is no more.

Double Trouble was scrapped in 1954, just months before the author was born. A memorandum from the Air Force Museum, responding to an inquiry about its status stated, "Sorry to have to tell you she doesn't exist anymore."

Charles A. Jones retired from the Marine Corps Reserve as a colonel in 2009, after serving a combination of 28 years on active duty and as a reservist. This is his first article for Air Force Magazine.

Glossary

ack-ack: Antiaircraft fire.

ammunition magazine: A room in which ammunition is kept in a ship.

AWOL: Absent without leave.

bivouac: A temporary encampment, often in an unsheltered area.

blister: A transparent bulge or dome on the fuselage of an airplane.

bloomers: Encasing for naval guns to shield gun crew from flash of powder.

chop-chop: Slang for food.

cowling: Metallic cover for an airplane engine.

coxswain: One who has charge of a boat, particularly its steering and navigation.

flak: Antiaircraft fire, especially as experienced by crews of combat airplanes.

glider: Special aircraft that has no engine.

hookman: One who operates a long hook to latch onto towlines or other crafts.

low-level mission: Flying at a low altitude—more susceptible to ground fire.

LST: Landing ship tank—carries vehicles, cargo, and troops onto unimproved shore.

machete: Large knife with broad blade used as weapon and to cut through vegetation.

merchant ship: Delivered troops and materials from North America to Britain.

MOS: Military occupation specialties.

Nazi: A German member of Adolph Hitler's political party.

NCO: Noncommissioned officer.

picket boat: A vehicle performing sentinel duty.

POW: Prisoner of war.

preparatory fire: Fire delivered on a target preparatory to an assault.

PX: Commissary on a United States Army post.

punji stick: Sharp bamboo stake concealed at an angle in high grass.

quads: Four guns in a single mounting.

ROTC: Reserve Officers' Training Corps.

R&R: Slang for rest and recuperation.

ruptured duck: Military service honorable discharge lapel pin—no longer given.

salvo: A simultaneous discharge of firearms in a battle.

scuttle: To sink by making holes in the bottom of the ship.

shell shock: Trauma suffered after serving on key battlefronts (World War I term).

summary execution: A person is killed on the spot without trial.

WAAC: Women's Auxiliary Army Corps.

wolf pack: Group of submarines that attack a single vessel or convoy.

zero: Japanese fighter plane.

Bibliography

"Battle of Iwo Jima." *Wikipedia*. Last modified January 17, 2011. http://en.wikipedia.org/wiki/Battle_of_iwo_jima.

"Battle of Okinawa." GlobalSecurity.org. Last modified April 26, 2005. http://www.globalsecurity.org/military/facility/okinawa-battle.htm.

"Battle of Saipan." *Wikipedia*. Last modified February 9, 2011. http://en.wikipedia.org/wiki/Battle-of-Saipan.

Chamberlain, Neville. "Peace in Our Time." Speech, September 30, 1938. *Britannia Historical Documents*. http://www.britannia.com/history/docs/peacetime.html.

Collins, William H. Interview on Audiotape with Ken Samuelson. June 6, 2006.

DuFore, Laura Mae. *A Life So Full*. Self-published, 2006.

"History of Veterans of America." Veterans of America. Last modified August 12, 2005. http://veterans-of-america.org/about_us.htm.

Lawson, James. Interview on Audiotape with Ken Samuelson, June 13, 2002.

Lord, Walter. *Day of Infamy*. New York: Henry Holt, 1957.

Louden, Teri. *On God's Wings*. Coronado, California: Louden Network, 2005.

"Malmedy Massacre." *Wikipedia*. Last modified January 30, 2011. http://en.wikipedia.org/wiki/malmedy_massacre.

Newman, Phil. Interview by Ken Samuelson, May 14, 1999.

Quillin, Martha. "He Shot Photos of the A-Bomb." *Charlotte Observer*, August 1, 2010.

"U.S. Merchant Marines in World War 11." American Merchant Marines at War. Last modified January 31, 2007. http://www.usmm.org/ww2.html.